Dud Dean

Dud Dean

MAINE GUIDE

Tales of Hunting and Fishing

By Arthur R. Macdougall, Jr.

Illustrated by Milton C. Weiler

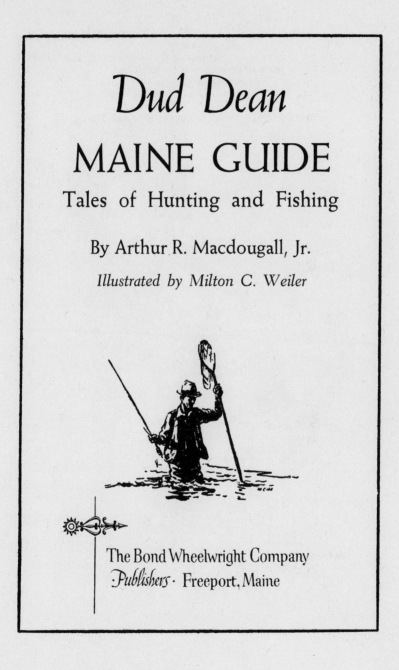

The Bond Wheelwright Company
Publishers · Freeport, Maine

CONTENTS

[vii]

INTRODUCTION

MOST of us do not read as we talk. We unconsciously conduct our reading as though we had never escaped from the classroom and the schoolmarm. That, one assumes, is not a misfortune, but it does impede the reader when he encounters dialect in print. Dialect isn't difficult, when one reads it as he talks, or at least as he has heard others speak.

When I began to write the Dud Dean stories, I prepared a dictionary of dialect, but I now doubt its usefulness as an instrument of precision. And I would go as far as Dr. George Philip Krapp goes in his most important work, *The English Language in America:* * "... all local dialects of this kind are at bottom merely general colloquial ... with a sprinkling of more characteristic words or pronunciations ... "

General dialect is born of the instinct of the race to say the thing as directly, briefly, and easily as possible. Vowels are slurred. "G's" are abandoned. For an example, Dud does not pronounce all the vowels in *should, would,* and *could.* Who does, except when making a conscious effort? Of course there are a few unusual pronunciations and words in Dud's speech. And there are grammatical independencies. If this were left to

* The Century Company, 1925.

[ix]

me, I would suggest that the purist in speech be permitted to throw the first, or fust, stone.

When a writer of stories like these attempts consistency of dialectic spelling, he is confronted with a double-barreled gun loaded with buckshot. In the first place such consistency will defeat his ambition to depict the living character, because the Dud Deans of real life are not consistent in their speech. They are not illiterate men. I have often heard Dud quote the careful speech of his wife, Nancy Dean, or some other person whose talk indicated a struggle against the laxity of common conversation. The dialect is not unmixed. Therefore it isn't consistently spoken. The second difficulty with slavish transcription arises in the reader's mind. He finds unusual phonetics laborious. The page appears to be cluttered with phonetic adaptations. Only an exceedingly clever writer could follow Dud in all his devices of speech and short cuts without perpetrating that which borders upon the ridiculous in print. For an example, Dud says "sunthin'" for *something*. He also pronounces *somehow*, "sunhow." But if one attempts a semblance of consistency, and writes "suntime" for *sometime*, the reader might become confused and miss the train...of thought.

The spelling of *you*, as Dud pronounces it, is "yer." It rimes with *her*, but is spoken with less emphasis. Dud slurs the pronoun. The "y" bears most of the burden. Yielding to an editor's insistence, I wrote "ye" instead of "yer" in many of these Dud Dean stories. The editor's contention was that "yer" would be confused with *your*. But since the possessive case is always set down in these stories as spelled by Webster, there need be no confusion.

Hereafter all editions of Dud Dean stories will cling to the genuine "yer," except where pronouncing this dialectic form in relation to a following word is difficult, when we shall avoid it as Dud avoids such difficulties.

Dud usually says "ter" for *to*. But the little word occurs so often on the printed page that it seems to trip the reader's attention. Therefore I have abandoned it.

The purpose to be achieved through the indicative use of this dialect as spoken by Dud and his fellows is to help the reader taste the salt and spice, the flavor, of the Upper Kennebec.

Dud Dean

I

DUD'S COUNTRY, ITS MEN
AND FISHERMEN

HAVING written this caption, I sit lost in reverie. I know
that I am alone in my study, and yet there are neighbors crowded
about my desk. They are looking over my shoulder at the white
paper and the pen in my hand. It is a moving experience, for
several of these familiar figures are not at beck and call. I have
seen them to their last resting place, where the Kennebec bounds
them on the west, and, flowing quietly, whispers to itself. These
have been precious years—the prime of life—but we had our
treasure in frail earthen vessels.

[3]

There are so many companionable voices that in the babel of pleasant distractions, I am at a loss to escape and to set about writing this chapter. Moreover, memories of rain-pelted or pleasant days are kaleidoscoped into this moment. And I am bemused. It is not easy to write about Dud's beloved country, and to refrain from personal interpolations. I will not attempt it.

I

To begin with, I have not seen the half of it. And yet, how many miles I have walked over disappearing tote roads, over vague trails, up hills and down, through tangles of alder and black growth and bog. And how many miles I have ridden, propelled by kickers and paddles. I can not name half the lakes I have fished, but if a roll were called of the waters in Dud's country, my visitations would seem to be hit or miss. I have fished little lakes as clear as mountain air, where one often "struck" before the trout reached the fly, because one could see them coming up at it in forty or fifty feet of water. I have angled in spring-fed bogs, full of dark, red-bellied trout, where the northern orchids and pitcher plants grow in the floating turf. I have cast over waters that were cradled on mountain tops. I have seen the trout fishing so easy and effortless that one tired of it—as a day on the Baker, when I took my limit of ten trout in four casts.

I have gunned for the ruffed grouse, keenest and finest of North American game birds, when we started flock after flock. I have set my hound into birch thickets for the varying hare, when four men could not cover the "rabbits" that emerged, casting off on their own. I have counted eighteen deer browsing within three hundred yards of our camp.

And, best of all, I have stood, casting from one spot on the bank of the Kennebec, and have taken the limit of that grand nonmigratory salmon that haunts those cold, clean waters.

Yes, these have been precious years. And little ragged memories come back to me of campfire narratives and lamplight yarns. Patches from some of these are stitched on the stories in this book, such as the evening fishing described in "Dark of the Moon."

Dud's country is a storied land from the days in the seventeenth century, when that half-fanatical Jesuit, Sebastian Ralé, came down the Kennebec to teach his self-sacrificial religion to the Abenaki. In October, 1775, Colonel Benedict Arnold's men came toiling through, on one of the most arduous marches in all history to attack one of the oldest cities in North America. Dud's country rang with their rabbled shouts and laughter.

The first map was made by Lieutenant John Montresor, a young engineer of the British Army. Montresor finished that map in 1761, after a canoe trip from Quebec, up the Chaudiere to the headwaters of the Penobscot, and down to a point where his Abenaki guides found the carry across the narrow divide to Moosehead Lake and the Kennebec waters. When he started home, having gone south as far as Fort Halifax, he followed the ancient Indian short cut across the Great Carry to Dead River. Following the West Branch of the Kennebec River, he came, at length, to the Height of Land, which he climbed to find his way back to Quebec. His ax blazes were still discernible on the carries, when Arnold came this way fourteen years later. Montresor had circled Dud's country. I would have liked to include a photocopy of that map in this book. The original is in the British Museum.

The Upper Kennebec is an immense country. It comprises

millions of acres. Those who are interested may find brief impressions of Dud's country in the journals of John Montresor, Benedict Arnold, Henry Dearborn, John Henry, and Doctor Isaac Senter. These, and others, are now gathered in one book: Kenneth Roberts' *March to Quebec*.

But these men, in Arnold's little army, found the wilderness pitted against them. There is no hint of the scale and grandeur of the land in their journals. They only saw the narrow fringe of forest along the waterways. And they saw that, when set upon by hurricane, flood, and winter. In that day, the northernmost settlement on the Kennebec was Norridgewock, a tiny outpost founded by William Warren and William Fletcher, of Concord, Massachusetts.

II

The first settlers found a dark, ancient forest of white pine, spruce, and hemlock. The rugged, laced and interlaced hills, which are the northern limits of the Appalachian Range, were clothed in sound and abundant timber.

The loggers came, when there were markets for the punkin pine and spruce. And the historian must reckon with the Upper Kennebec, and the almost endless millions of saw logs which these hardy men drove down the many tributaries; sent roaring down and grinding down from the hills and plateaus above the East and West Branches.

The men of the Upper Kennebec move against this background. They should be distinguished from the peripatetic loggers who came in droves to work for the famous bosses. Of course these loggers left their marks upon the Upper Kennebec. There are granite ledges along the riverbanks that are worn by their innumerable calked boots. Baker calks. These wandering loggers were four-meal-a-day specimens. Kendrick Burns, of the S. D. Warren Company, put it, "One doesn't find any gilded geraniums in the woods."

The Upper Kennebec Valley bred a race of men who shared in the exploits of brawn and daring with Stewart Holbrook's *Holy Old Mackinaw* type, but were not of their ilk. The wandering loggers may have terrified the clerks and women, when they went to town, but Dud's kind spat on their hands, and took the hell-raisers' measurements, if they were so unwise as to insist upon it. The men of Dud's country owned their homes along the river valley. They were family men, and proud of it. They went into the woods for the winter, and they came out in the spring with their wages in their breeches pockets.

There was a manhood in them that almost matched the giant pines. And if they sometimes swore oaths that were as sharp as January mornings, they also paid their "just debts, one hundred cents on the dollar."

Black growth spells the wildlands. Men cut roads through it; fall the somber pines and spruce, but it lays its spell upon them. I stood on a sidewalk in Bingham, while John Kelly reproduced, to the best of his vocal ability, the *mysterious voice* of the Enchanted. A hundred men, all in the prime of life, heard that weird cry one winter night, some fifty years ago. They went out with lanterns and searched from the landing at Dead River for miles around, and found no human tracks in the new snow.

I would not smile at John Kelly. Not I. He remembered how

men sometimes felt, when they went to cut the punkin pine on the Enchanted, and all such awesome stands of virgin timber. It was a wilderness that dwarfed the statures of the men who went to despoil it. They got the pine down to the mills, but the wilderness set her mark upon them. You and I may doubt that his Satanic Majesty danced on a camp roof, while the men were eating supper, but we were not there.

That which is sugar and salt to a man of parts may be poison to a man of lesser breed. But this flavoring of the supernatural kept life from becoming unbearably flat and monotonous. That was its justification, and enough. The bill of fare was molasses, pork, and beans. The camps were "low-posted," close, and effluvial. Working hours were from before dawn until after dark. Nothing less than the Devil, dancing on the camp roof, could break the grip of such monotony.

And there was humor. Poetry and humor are born of the same quality of mind. So Shakespeare is, perhaps, the greatest of our poets. Poetry and humor, at their best, are therapeutic. I offer one anecdote which is a gem as an example of humor at work, leavening the lump. The story goes that so-and-so climbed into his bunk at the end of one of those herculean days. He lit his pipe and smoked a while. Then he put it aside, and fell asleep. When called in the dark of the next morning, he grabbed his pipe and dragged upon it with elaborate earnestness. "By gob," he exclaimed, "it *has* gone out."

A few readers have referred to Dud as a crude character. If the adjective is justified, I have bungled the chronicle. Dud's kind are not crude. Perhaps the judgment was based upon a superficial taste for grammarisms.

III

Fresh-water fish were once an essential in diet. Early settlers on the Upper Kennebec smoked and salted trout and salmon for winter food. The Kennebec River was one of the finest salmon rivers in the United States. *Salmo salar*, the Atlantic salmon, fought his way up over every riff and fall in the river. Thousands of tons of that splendid fish crowded the tributary streams all the way from Augusta tidewater to the forks of the river, and on up both branches. The Kennebec would still be among the salmon rivers, but for the dams, which, beginning with the dam at Augusta, are barriers preventing the wealth and the health of the sea access to the river.

At any rate, angling was once a part-time occupation, which modern vocations and industry have crowded to the seacoast, where it is still an economic enterprise. Here, inland, angling for fish is only an ancient instinct and an epicurean avocation. He who matches the worth of his trout, say, at the price of mackerel, with the cost of his rod and tackle plus the value of his time, will learn that fishing is expensive. That being true, and if one be of a miserly mood, he should forego the unlucrative business.

But the men of the Upper Kennebec do not count the cost— it being relatively unimportant. The love of this sport is in them from the beginning and will be until the end. Colonel Benedict Arnold found time to write in his diary for Wednesday, October 11, 1775: "... here our People [soldiers of the expedition] caught a prodigious number of fine Salmon Trout [*Salvelinus frontinalis*], nothing being more common than a man's taking 8 or 10

[9]

Doz in one hours time, which generally weigh half a pound a piece."

Dud remembers fishing like that at East Carry Pond, where Arnold wrote that note in his diary. And those half-pounders were "little" trout compared to those that toured the Kennebec! It is still good trout fishing at East Carry and in the Kennebec. How could a man get such fishing out of mind! No wonder Dud and his countrymen esteem this charr: the dark-backed, tourmaline-spotted, rinsed-in-wet-gold-dust trout.

But the trout must share the laurel with the nonmigratory salmon, *Salmo salar sebago*. This is the prince of all fresh-water fishes. Pound for pound, or anyway one compares him with other fish, even with the lashing, smashing bass, this is the peerless species. Like the famed ouananiche of the St. John's region, this is a nonmigratory salmon. That is, its lifetime is spent in fresh water. Unlike the salmon of the sea, it never seeks the lushness of salt-water food.

This nonmigratory salmon is often called "the landlocked salmon." The theory behind that misnomer is that these fish originated when their forebears (ocean salmon spawning in fresh water) were landlocked, or trapped, by some ancient geological barrier, or, later, by man-made dams. But, either way, that is a most improbable hypothesis. Certainly this species originated ages before men built dams—anywhere. And the notion that geological barriers prevented the return of the salmon to the sea is ill considered, because water flows around or over barriers. That would prevent the origin of a nonmigratory salmon, since the fish would be free to go down to the sea, but unable to return above the obstruction.

Salmo salar sebago is a Maine-born fish. It was originally found in a few lakes. Now it has been widely distributed throughout the state. In Sebago Lake, one of the original waters, it achieved its proudest proportions and vigor. Fortunately, one of the first specimens to be examined by a competent ichthyologist came from Sebago. Hence the tag: *Salmo salar sebago*.

The nonmigratory salmon is a hungry feeder. His smashing, leaping tactics often free him from the novice's fly, and not infrequently from the seasoned angler's hook.

Although this fish strikes freely at trolled spoons, baited with smelt, shiners, or "nightwalkers," I have learned from Dud to feel it is a shame to take so game a fish on heavy tackle.

Let a man go after him with lighter equipment, and he will be rewarded. Although this fish often takes the fly with abandon, he is more exclusive than the trout. The anglers up in Dud's country go after salmon and trout with streamer and bucktail flies, and with smaller wet and dry fly patterns. The streamer fly is tied in many patterns, and new ones appear each year, but the imitation of small fishes is its basic principle. Most of us have learned to vary our methods, when fishing with streamers. This fly may be fished up or down the current, brought home with erratic or swift, straight runs. The latter are accomplished by rapidly stripping the line or by reel. Probably there are more salmon taken in this way than any other method of casting. The point is, of course, that the streamer resembles a minnow, and that it loses all resemblance, when permitted to sag or rest in the water.

The following list includes the flies most commonly used in Dud's country. Some of these patterns are equally attractive to salmon and trout. A few have been tied for one species. The letters T or S indicate for trout or salmon, while TS or ST indicate that both trout and salmon take the fly—it being, however, somewhat more successful for the first.

Streamers and Bucktails

Black Ghost	ST	Grey Ghost	ST
Mickey Finn	TS	Lady Ghost	ST
Col. White and Dana	S	Silver Doctor	S
Several streamers which are predominantly green:		The Trout Rocks, particularly No. 2.	T
The 9-3	S	Lady Doctor	T
Nimrod	ST	Edison Tigers	TS
Green Ghost, etc.	S	Supervisor	ST
Gaddis	S	Red White Polar Bear	TS
Bolshevik	TS	Moose River	ST
Warden's Worry	TS	Royal Coachman	TS

The Old Dependable Wets, Eights and Tens

Montreals	TS	Jock Scott	ST
Dark		Dusty Miller	ST
White Tipped		Hare Ear	TS
Light		Brown Hackle	TS
Yellow		Cahill	TS
Parmacheene	T	Grey Hackle	TS
Cow Dung	S	Grizzly King	TS
Black Gnat	ST	March Brown	TS
Black Ant	ST	Professor	T
Caddis	TS	Coachman	T
Silver Doctor	ST	Ibis	T

Dud's friends use dry flies, when the wets fail. I do not know a man in this country who might be classed as a dry-fly purist. When using the dry fly, Kennebecers seek to match the hatch, for it is during the hatch that the wet fly fails, and the trout and salmon become addicted to a particular natural fly. Among the dry flies, I think of but one exception to this rule of "match the hatch." The Fan Wing Coachman is usually magic on the Kennebec. I use it anytime the fishing lags, hatch or no hatch. A Number Eight seems to be more effective than a smaller size.

Years ago, probably as soon as Dud's friends became acquainted with the dry fly, they began to use dry flies while lake and pond fishing. Why not? Many flies hatch in pond water—the May flies, for example. When wet flies failed, the question was, "Why not try one of them newfangled dry flies?" The fact that dry flies were traditionally fished up a stream didn't count with Dud's friends. Trout were feeding on a hatch. They needed a fly that would float naturally, and that resembled the natural fly as much as possible. Thus began the most enjoyable of all lake fishing. The dry fly worked.

My neighbors are adept at catching fish. The skills of some of them are uncanny! The secret seems to be that they do not concentrate on technique. They are only intent on *how* to get that fish. And so they are always changing their fishing tactics, suiting the angling to the immediate problem.

I think that the most important point Dud's friends have to teach many a tourist fisherman is the way to wade the river. They are careful to fish from the shore, before wading out into the water. Thus they avoid putting many a trout and salmon out and away. And when wading, they move with caution to

avoid rolling rocks on the bottom. Why a fish scares, or is not frightened, is something to guess about, but the basic rule is to play it safe.

From four- to six-ounce rods are used. Lighter rods are not used, because backbone is necessary when one is casting streamers. Lines are chosen with much care. Leaders are selected to fit the fishing. Waders are regarded as an imported luxury, associated, Amos-wise, with those who eat the fatted calf, and cannot take it, because of a soft life.

However, the waters are cold, and one sometimes wishes he had a fat calf to swap for waders.

II

THE ANGLER FROM ATHENS

AT CERTAIN camps on Moosehead, I found that Dud was out with a party of "sporters," as summer vacationists are called up in Maine. It was four o'clock, and I had two hours to spend as best I could. Moosehead is an inland sea, some forty miles long. In June a fisherman can pick up trout anywhere, but I did not feel inclined to strike out alone. After all, good company is half, or more than that, of the fishing trip.

So I wandered down to the stone wharf and sat down. There is a fine joy to be extracted from meditation in a place like that.

Farm Island, wooded with a mixed growth, lies to the south of Tomhegan Point. Its acreage would fill up the average-sized lake. Moosehead was in a tranquil mood that afternoon—blue and lovely as a fairy mirror. One could feel a lull in time and place. The spirit of it soaked into one's heart. It gripped the lake and all the country round about.

Probably I had been sitting there for half an hour, when a rather large-sized pattern of a man came down from the camps and parked himself alongside. We nodded, but I was of a mind to continue my reveries. After a few moments the newcomer cleared his throat:

"Stayin' here?"

It was a reasonable question, and deserved an answer, so I replied, "No. Are you?"

"Nope. Jist up here on a little business. I live down ter Athens —Athens, Maine."

Evidently we were neighbors, Athens and Bingham being situated in the same section of Somerset County. In an unguarded moment, I admitted my own residence.

"Pshaw, I wanter know! Now ain't that a sight? Up here fishin'?"

"Not yet."

"Well, ain't that curious? I was jist wishin' that I'd brought my pole, an' a good can of worms. My wife said I'd better. But I says to her, 'I'm goin' up thar on business, an' ain't got no time fer no fumdiddling.' Suppose we c'ud dig some worms 'round here?"

The proposition didn't interest me. I don't fish with worms for the simple reason that I find it dull sport, when trout will take flies. And I was probably about to say something of the sort, when a voice said, "Howdy, Mak."

It was Dud, who had been quietly paddling up the shore.

"Hello, Dud! How they rising?"

"Not bad. Want to try 'em after supper?"

I glanced at the citizen from Athens. He was opening his mouth. I headed him off.

"Sorry, but you see I already have a date for some fly fishing."

"Shucks," said the man from Athens, "don't mention that. I'd jist soon go fishin' with three as two. Yer won't mind takin' me 'long, will yer?"

Dud looked him over, a quiet smile playing about his mouth. "Got any rig?" he asked.

"No. But by Judas, I'll git one off'n somebudy."

Whereupon, the man from Athens jumped to his feet, dusting off his trousers with a pair of hands large enough to get anything gettable. When the fellow had departed in search of his rig, I exploded, "Say, it's my guess that we don't want that fellow. Fishing is a democratic sport, to be sure, but it isn't necessarily permixtive."

Dud chuckled. "Maybe he won't find it so easy to borrow, up here."

Well, we didn't see anything of Barns—that was his name, it seemed—during the supper hour, and I began to breathe easily. Dud had been around to tip off the rod owners. "I sh'udn't be surprised if he found it difficult to borrow a rod," he said with a grin.

We lost no time after supper. June evenings are long, but not long enough, when the lake lies splashed with color and deep with shadow. It is something to have lived and fished in an hour like that.

I was stowing away my gear, when a loud voice called, "Hey thar! Hold up!"

We had almost forgotten Athens, but her delegate was coming on the run. And in his right hand was a rod stiff enough to lift a tarpon.

"What d'yer know," he said, "that cook tried to tell me that he hadn't any pole—tried to hold out on me, that's what. Lucky I see it behind the door. But thar ain't a worm to be had, so they claim. So I get me a bunch of flies off the cook. He says that any damn fool can use 'em. Where yer want me to set?"

I started to say, "In the middle of the lake," but Dud laughed, and pointed to the widest part of his canoe.

"Know anythin' erbout a canoe?" he asked, as the man from Athens sat down.

"No, but I've rid the logs."

"Guess yer'll do, then."

The rod that Barns had "borrowed" was too stiff for fly fishing, but so was he. Discovering his difficulties, he developed a technique of his own. He would sling the line underhand, backward as far as possible. Then, after the flies had settled on the lake, he would make a forward pass. The result was an annoying "plop" each time he lifted the leader on the forward sling. It really sounded as though the leader were glued down, and had to be ripped up every time he brought it forward. Barns bulked so large that I could not see Dud, but I heard a chuckle now and then.

At the start, that night, the fish seemed to be on a vacation.

THE ANGLER FROM ATHENS

"Dad-burn a pond as big as this one," grumbled Barns. "I bet the trout are lost half the time. I bet—"

He had put on three flies selected, apparently, for their color. It would be fun to watch Barns select neckties for himself. When he broke off his "betting," a little half-pound trout had appeared and had made a pass at his assortment. Whereupon, with an astonishing dexterity, Barns yanked the whole outfit from the little chap's reach.

"Didjer see that?" he demanded. "Thar was a dandy two-pounder nibbled at my flies, but he missed 'em somehow."

Dud chuckled.

Actually, Barns managed to return his flies within eight feet of the strike. "Thar, by Judus Priest, try that caper ag'in. Hump!"

The trout did try again, in halfhearted fashion, but thereafter tried it no more.

"If I jist had me a good can of worms—"

"Try letting your flies sink," I suggested, having only in mind that he might possibly hook one that way.

Barns glared at me suspiciously.

"Don't yer know no better'n that?" he demanded sternly. "The idee is to keep them floatin'. Yer don't let 'em sink. Yer kind of skitter 'em, like yer had a hunk of salt pork on, an' was skitterin' fer pickerel."

And, as if he felt that more were necessary, he added, "I thought you was a fisherman."

"I don't pretend to know a thing about it," I said, rather stiffly.

More chuckles from Dud in the stern.

[21]

"I kin see yer ain't used to fly fishin', anyway," continued Barns. "Now if yer'd jist try sluggin' your flies out back, like I'm doin', and then fetch 'em up front, where ye're aimin', yer'd git out more line, even with that dinkly little pole."

But Barns had to turn his attention to his own fishing. That little acrobatic trout was back again. The man from Athens missed again. And when next the trout appeared, it hit my fly. Dud netted him; took the hook lightly out of the fish's mouth, and returned it to the water. Barns stared. It was evident that he thought Dud was loony.

"Got another of them yeller an' black flies?" he asked.

I handed him a western bee.

"Now here goes," he said.

We were working down to the end of Farm Island. Then we swung off, heading for Tomhegan Cove. The citizen from Athens was the first to spot the togue. "Look at that!" he shouted.

About fifty feet ahead of us, something was cutting the surface of the lake like a slowly drawn knife. The lake was dead calm, and there was no mistaking the motion. And as we watched, another and then another back fin appeared.

"Crotch," whispered Barns, "be them pickerel?"

"Togue," said Dud. "But we can't run any closer, er they'll strike off fer parts unknown. I'll ease up, far's I can. The trick is to put your flies jist in front of 'em. But the fust thing, my fat friend, is to take off that string of millinery. Take 'em off, an' put on *one* dark fly."

Barns began to paw around in the cook's flybook for a dark fly.

THE ANGLER FROM ATHENS

Before us was some fly fishing to remember. Togue are, of course, deep-water fish. Once in the moons of June, one might hope to find the big fish cruising about on the surface in this fashion. Few and fortunate are the anglers who have found the togue in a fly-taking mood. And to that auspicious moment, God might add the silence of the majestic evening, the patches of yellow light from a low, round sun, and the faraway indistinct sounds of the woods.

Dud slid the canoe within a reasonable cast of a black fin. I confess to have been too anxious to get in my own fly, while the guy from Athens was arranging his leader for action. To my chagrin, the fly fell two feet short of the objective. The big fish submerged. But there were more fish on the surface. At the next try—a long cast—the fly landed two feet ahead of the periscope.

The old boy saw the fly on the instant, and started full speed ahead, smashing it with a vicious crack. The water boiled for a moment. Then down he went. And the old timer took a pile of line before he began to sulk.

Then the battle began in earnest. At first, he sullenly refused to budge. After that he began to lash about at a depth of fifty feet. But all his tactics, although courageous and never once tame, were dogged rather than spectacular. For all I could tell, it might have been a monster squaretail.

I think that I hurried him too much, when he came to the surface, after considerable use of the reel. Dud missed him with the gaff, and the fish swung off again. Finally I worked him in, and Dud's neat pass with the gaff landed the fish in the canoe.

"Now, by Crimminy," shouted the man from Athens, "let me have a chance!"

"Set down!" said Dud, in a level voice.

He sat down, but continued to plead to be paddled nearer to the zone of sporting togue. I waited. In fact there was nothing else to do but to wait and dodge. Waiting was not easy. Those big fellows were drifting here and there—zigzag or straight ahead —five pounds, ten pounds, twenty pounds—how much bigger, one could not tell.

"Look at that one," wailed Barns. "It's as big as a stick of pulpwood! What a fish! Oh, by Judas Priest!"

And as Barns fished, he waxed to stronger language—or weaker, depending upon one's point of view. He talked, as he fished, spectacularly, but out of control. There were contrasts. A late, blue haze hung over the lake. The shoreline was darkened to a smudge, and the peacefulness that one can not barter nor buy hung over the lake. It hung over Barns, but he did not seem to sense it.

If he hadn't been so self-isolated in his own side show, he would have sat down for a moment, at least. Dud did not ask him to sit again, and I concluded that Dud hoped the man would fall in the lake. Meanwhile, we ducked and dodged the wildly flung fly from the end of Barns's rod. Dud pulled his hat brim down over his eyes, and I considered putting my head between my knees. The air was a-whistle. I thought of Will Rogers' lariat.

And the togue? They continued to cruise where they willed, blissfully unaware of our ambitions. There were times when a Simple Simon could have hooked one. At last a lordly old fellow swirled toward the canoe.

"Put it in front of him," directed Dud. "An' if yer muff this fish, ye're done fer the evenin'. Mak an' me 'ud like some fishin'. As 'tis, a man might's well try castin' long side of a windmill."

Barns tried, no doubt, but his fly landed ten feet behind the fish, which continued on his way. But the man from Athens was not done. He cast again and succeeded, by a tremendous fluke, in placing his fly in front of the departing fish. The magnificent fish charged! Whang! It was a strike to end all strikes. It was masterly. And the old laker knew it. He dug for the bottom of Moosehead. At every turn, he went down two contours. Now if Barns had been able to get his big thumb inside that reel, I am sure that he would have saved a whole lot of the cook's line. Of course he tried to halt the flow of line, but that big fish had a start on him. Finally he caught hold of the line with his left hand and started lifting with his right.

"Don't do that!" warned Dud. "Let him have plenty of line. He'll stop!"

"By the tar an' feathers of Marblehead, I don't believe he ever intends to stop!"

"If you try to stop him, now, you'll smash the cook's rod, or lose his line," I butted in.

"Crotch a-mighty! D'yer think I'm a lunkhead? Puff—puff. Don't yer think I know how to handle a fish? I—"

The heavy rod was bent in an arch. Suddenly it gave way with a sickening snap. For a few moments that togue got all the line he wanted—probably a hundred feet of it.

But Barns slammed the rod into the canoe, knocking my hat off into the lake. The line hung over the gunwale, slack and idle. He closed his big hands over it, then gingerly reached for it at the

[25]

water level. Dud thrust his paddle deeply, and saved us all from a thorough wetting. And the man from Athens, heedless, began dragging in the line, hand over hand. It came easily at first, as though the laker had shaken the hook. But it finally tightened with a yank, and the wet line slid through his hands like a snake.

After that Barns was in earnest. Of course that gamy old veteran at the bottom of the lake was hooked hard. And little by little, he was forced to give ground. There was a stiff go, now and then, but Barns wasn't giving any quarter. At last he got the fish to the canoe.

"Hand me a net!" he yelled.

Now it happened that there was a net in the canoe—a net that was far too small for such a fish. There was a gaff. But Barns had demanded a net, so he got it. Puffing and hissing between clinched teeth, like a spent runner of ancient Athens at the close of one of those classic marathons, Barns made a scoop at the togue with the little net. He succeeded in getting part of the laker into it. It flopped powerfully. The big fly tore loose, and Barns' fish fell back into Moosehead. He made one silly and futile scoop, before the fish disappeared—back up, tail slowly fanning.

There was a momentous pause, and then Dud Dean spoke: "That's a good job. I'm glad of it."

"Amen," said I.

The night had been lingering afar off. Perhaps it had been watching what would surely have been a comedy, but for the valor of the togue. Anyhow, we suddenly saw that it was nearly dark. And away off somewhere I thought I heard Something bigger and wiser than Dud, or the angler from Athens, or myself, say:

"AMEN!"

But the angler from Athens said something else.

III

DARK OF THE MOON

DUD DEAN and I sat on a stick of pulpwood that had been cut from the butt of a giant spruce. It was about six o'clock in the evening. We had been discussing the prospects, but had lapsed into silence.

"Waiting for a hatch?" asked a voice.

Dud and I turned. There stood a young man whose every grace and garment betrayed him as a visitor. I was a little disturbed, for we had been waiting for the hour when we were to undertake some private fishing. But Dud's face wrinkled amiably.

"No," he answered, "jist waitin' fer the dark of the moon."

"That sounds jolly," declared the stranger. "Are there browns in this river?"

"Nope. They're pink, mostly."

"Oh, I see. When you mentioned the moon, I thought of brown trout. Browns feed at night."

"Aya? So do pinks."

"Were you serious about the dark of the moon?"

"Jist as serious as an almanac," Dud assured the young man.

The stranger sat down. A moment of silence followed. That is, we were quiet. The Kennebec continued its whispering along the shore. A merganser flew downstream, no more than a foot above the tumbling water. And off across the river, under the yellow haze of the late afternoon, a hermit thrush began to sing.

The young man spoke:

"Mind if I stay a while?"

"Crotch, no," said Dud, genuinely astonished at the question. "Like I hinted, we're waitin' fer the evenin' fishin'."

"Pink trout?" asked the stranger, with a grin.

"Nope. That is, we're kinda figgerin' on some salmon."

"Salmon! Why, that's what I really came up here to catch. There's a fellow who lives up this way somewhere who occasionally writes about these nonmigratory salmon. He has made some extravagant claims concerning their fighting powers. But say, perhaps you know him. I can't seem to recall his name, but it's Mac-something-or-other."

The stranger and I were looking at Dud. I wondered if the visitor noticed a set of little wrinkles that danced, momentarily, at the outer corners of Dud's eyes.

"Yer say this writin' feller's name begins with Mac?" drawled Dud. "Seems so I sh'ud know him if he lives round here."

The stranger was helpful. "Oh, well," he said. "I dare say he's obscure. You know, small stuff. But—say, you should know the old codger he writes about. He is supposed to be a guide up in this neck of the woods."

"How *old* would yer say he is?" asked Dud. "Older'n I be?"

"Oh, gosh, yes. A regular old hayseed. The natives up here do talk a little after the fashion, but this old cuss simply murders the king's English."

The wrinkles danced again about Dud's eyes. "I dunno. I'd kinda hate to admit that I knew all the guides up in our country."

The stranger nodded his head. "It's probable that this old cuss is fictitious, anyway."

"Wel-el, I dunno but if I was you I'd be careful erbout callin' some of our guides *that* name. What's this writin' chap look like? Got any idea?"

"No, come to think of it, I never did see a picture of him."

"What's he write about? Maybe we can git a slant on that."

"Oh, nothing in particular. Just the usual line of stuff."

"I getcha," said Dud. "Yer mean, if he knew as much as he confesses to know, he'd be old Izaak Walton hisself in a one-piece bathin' suit."

The stranger chuckled. "I'll say!"

I may have been laboring under an unjustifiable impulse, but it seemed to be my turn. "This *old* cuss you mentioned. It seems to me that we should be able to place *him*."

The stranger broke into laughter. Apparently something had pleased him. For an uneasy moment I was apprehensive.

"Say!" he exclaimed. "In a sense, that old codger must be priceless. I'd give a five-dollar bill to meet him—you know, string him along. That is, if he isn't just a wild figment of this guy's imagination."

"Crotch," muttered Dud, pulling at one end of his mustache. "Crotch, figment!"

"You know," said the stranger hurriedly, "it reads somewhat like the natives talk—er—er, illiterate."

"The natives is all dead an' gone in this country," commented Dud. "They spoke Injun."

"Hold on. I don't mean to be offensive. Every section has its dialect, more or less. I dare say that my talk places me."

"Crotch, son, don't be upset. Anyhow, the sun's gone down behind Fletcher Mountain. Let's git ourselves together. Fish'll be jumpin'."

So we began to gather our duffel.

"Neighbor," said Dud, turning to me, "how about some of them worms, or have yer used them all up?"

"Worms!" exclaimed the stranger.

"Aya. Little pinkish critters, about four inches long."

The stranger was obviously shocked. His eyes wandered uncertainly to Dud's old felt hat, which sported a considerable array of flies—both wet and dry. Dud knew that the old hat had given him the lie.

"I think you are trying to pull my leg."

Dud chuckled. "Hope not, young feller. But I'm afraid my friend, here, has used up all the worms. Don't it beat the old devil hisself how hard it is to find 'em durin' dry weather?"

"I wouldn't know," said the stranger, taking an elaborate dry-fly kit from a spacious jacket pocket and proceeding to select a light Cahill.

"Purty delicate-lookin'," commented Dud.

"I'm sticking to them," said the stranger a little stiffly, and he waded out into the river until the water was up to his belt.

"That little joke about the worms kinda turned on me," said Dud as we walked down the river to the point we had intended to fish. "Now that I've got rid of him, what do ye think of yourself?"

I didn't commit myself on that point.

"Reckon life's a purty short wrastle."

I continued running my line through the guides.

"Somethin' funny 'bout the bottom up thar where he's fishin'. Never is no trout up thar. Mak, guess I'll go have a talk with that city cuss. Might's well, don't yer think?"

"Sure."

Presently I heard him addressing the man who was casting a neat line out into the tinted water of the Kennebec.

"Better come along with us. We ain't cherubs—at least my friend ain't—but it happens that worms go 'plop' when a feller throws 'em in, an' that wouldn't work tonight. As a matter of fact, ye've sort of walked into somethin'. This is purty special fishin'. Me an' that long-legged feller has always kept it private. But we ain't so mean as to cut off our noses to spite our faces; so we're goin' to let yer in on it, as Barb Baker said, the time he strapped a tramp in the tramp-chair."

The stranger reeled in his line and waded toward Dud.

"An' so," continued Dud, "you do promise to take this fishin' danged serious an' to keep it as private as an empty barn. By no slip of the tongue or lapse of memory, or rash deed of good fellowship are yer to confide, share, will, bequeath, or otherwise let slip this secret, so help yer. Understand?"

"To tell the truth," said the stranger, with an open grin, "I don't understand a thing—not a thing—but I'll see you through, if for no other reason than to satisfy myself that either you're crazy or I'm demented."

"All right," agreed Dud.

When they reached the point, where I was already casting, the stranger said:

"Why, man, we've passed by better-looking water than this."

"No, we ain't," contradicted Dud. "Handsome is as handsome ain't. Now listen to me. I've seen folks that considered themselves quite some anglers spoil the fishin' in a place like this; so yer listen to me.

"To begin with, we stand as far back from this water as we can git, an' not git tangled on the backcast. We put on one fly —a nymph—like this. We cast out as far as we can at fust. As darkness creeps on we shorten our casts, becuz these salmon work their way from the deeper water to feed in these shallows along this bar. If we don't git a strike by the time it takes the fly to settle about six inches, we ease it up to the surface, an' take it away with as little ruction as is possible.

"When we have to step round in these roundish rocks, that roll an' clank agin' each other, we do it jist as carefully as possible. As dark comes, it's all right to move up nearer the river. Then ye'll be using a short line, not castin' more'n ten or twelve feet from the edge. Git it?"

[34]

"I don't see how a man can handle a fish—even a small fish—in such shallow water after darkness."

Dud chuckled. "Jist wait an' see. Matter of fact, these fish run fer fast water at the prick of the hook. That makes it easy."

So we spread out, about fifty feet apart, and began the fishing that has always been the most exciting and delightful of all the angling I have experienced. Some time passed, during which male lightning bugs took up their twinkling search for lovers in the interval grass behind us. Then katydids took up the vindictive argument of long standing, and finally we heard the stranger's voice:

"Say, I've been casting here, in the same spot, for twenty minutes. What next?"

"Crotch, young feller," called Dud, "yer rest the water fer a few minutes. Then yer go after your fish some more."

A whippoorwill began calling through the night. A large bug, probably a belated June bug, went buzzing and booming by my ear. And I rested the water out in front of me, as Dud had advised the stranger to do. When I began casting again, the river, which still reflected the uncertain afterglow, exploded about eight feet from the shore line in front of the stranger, who was now a black silhouette.

"Golly!" I heard him exclaim, and knew that he had missed the strike.

"Did you see that?" he called to me.

"I heard it. They're quick; but don't miss as a rule."

He called again: "This is queer fishing. I haven't seen a sign of a fish feeding on the surface."

"They're feeding on nymphs."

The stranger lit a cigar.

"Guess I'd be careful of a light," called Dud.

The lighted cigar was hastily abandoned.

"Talkin' is almost as bad," concluded Dud.

The stranger chuckled.

And in a moment a rock that one could not have put in a bushel basket seemed to explode in my face—well, almost in my face. I had been casting at that rock. And I felt the salmon roll as I set the hook. A second later there was a white streak, drawn perpendicularly above the black level river.

There is, or so it has always seemed to me, a nervous exaltation to this night fishing that tops all other angling. One's hands are busy when a big salmon hitches on to a light leader. And one's hands must be his eyes for the most part. It has amused me to speculate on what those gentlemen who maintain that a taut line is not essential would do under such circumstances. I do not mean to make night fishing sound too difficult. It isn't. It is simply a matter of keeping busy after the manner one has thoroughly learned while fishing in daylight.

When I landed this salmon, the stranger said, "I'd give ten dollars to hook one of those babies."

The night sounds, of which I had been oblivious for the past fifteen minutes, began again. It was dark indeed. The water out in front of us had lost all definition. One could not see where his fly was landing. We moved toward the edge of the river, until we stood within five or six feet of the water. Stars hung over us and were reflected in the current. The river murmured in an older tongue than I understood, but the sound was pleasant.

Then the stranger hooked two salmon in succession. He lost

the first at the end of a lot of line. But he landed the second, and his voice was oddly vibrant for that of a man who must have taken many bigger fish under other circumstances.

"Man!" he exclaimed. "These fish are made of steel springs!"

I wondered about Dud, for I knew that he had elected the least likely stand along this little stretch of water. Within five minutes the stranger hooked another fish. I heard it spank the water several times and heard the soft metallic sound of his reel as his line ran out and out. Presently his activities ceased and all was quiet. Then I heard him muttering in surprise, and then in a louder voice he informed me that the son-of-a-seacook had given him the slip.

And it was about that moment that a smashing strike came to me. It was a big salmon! I had him in hand for a moment or two; but instead of cutting for the deeper water, he wallowed like a trapped muskrat. And the line went slack.

"Holy Moses!" said the stranger.

"Sounded old-fashioned," commented Dud, after which he whistled a snatch of tune.

The stranger hooked and landed another salmon. "Lacks a little of being fourteen inches," he said, and returned it to the river.

"Kinda sad," said Dud, "but I'm afeared our time is shrinkin'."

Off on the mountain to the west a weird, unmistakable call disturbed the peace of the night. It came to us again, and then again, as though much farther away.

"What in damnation!" exclaimed the stranger.

As I opened my mouth to inform him a commotion, similar to the racket that had occurred at the end of my line but a few moments before, erupted at the end of Dud's line. And, like an entranced man, I responded with the word that had been half formed on my lips:

"Bear!"

"Huh?" Since the stranger's mind was by that time fixed upon the explosion down in Dud's position, his voice sounded absolutely incredulous.

"Clean the decks fer action," called Dud. "I've got somethin' here that is goin' to lick me, if he can. So if I have to head up your way, move back before I trumple on yer. Whoap!"

Something that sounded as big as a medium-sized stick of pulpwood fell smack on the river. And in an instant it fell again. Then again.

"Boy!" drawled Dud. "What if we never git a look at that fish! Who's goin' to restrain our imaginations?"

The stranger came stumbling down to me and I began to like him, because he seemed too excited to talk coherently. Twice blessed is the man who is genuinely enthusiastic over a fish at the end of the other fellow's line!

Dud's reel, which sings musically, ran out and out. And soon Dud was following the salmon out on the last little point of rocks. But he could not stop there, and soon stood in the water to his belt.

"Crotch a-mighty, if this fish happens to ask fer more line, you fellers will probably never see me ag'in. Tell Nancy that I jist went off over my head, a-followin' a crazy salmon. Jumpin' horn pouts! Thar he goes ag'in—right 'cross current. An' he's got every danged inch of line, upon my soul. Thar! Hear him jump? Crotch! Thar he goes ag'in."

Then I remembered my flashlight. When the salmon jumped again, at the end of Dud's line, my flashlight picked him out—straight up in the air.

The stranger gasped.

"I'll never forget that picture as long as I live. Talk about beauty! My gosh, my gosh! It's as though we were watching a ghostly fish battling on the end of an HDH line. Whew!"

A few moments passed, and the stranger grasped my shoulder. "I wonder if you realize," he shouted in my ear, "that this friend of yours is probably the best man with a rod in the whole world?"

Somehow it didn't occur to me that he was possibly putting it too strongly.

Dud was able to emerge and to stand in knee-deep water. "He's buckin' the current," the old master informed us. "Now he's slicin' it sideways, puttin' all the downhill drag he can on me, the old cuss. If I don't git him back on this side of the river before long, we're never goin' to see him! This is the best fish I ever hooked. I never see nothin' like him, except a hoss mackerel that was hangin' up in a Portland fish market. I told Nancy at the time, 'That mackerel is almost as big as a salmon I hooked up to Pierce Pond.' An' she says, 'You should be 'shamed!'

"Thar! Watch him. He's jumpin' ag'in. Hear him hit the water, tryin' to foul my leader. Thar, yer p'ison son of a Jezreelite, how's that feel? Never thought thar was so much life in the old rod, did yer? Yer thought—Thar he goes up the river, hell-bent fer election! You fellers git out of the way. I can't turn out fer nothin'."

The stranger and I followed with the flashlight. Then it seemed as though Dud had taken complete command of the situation.

"Jist let him try that caper a few times, an' he's my fish—that is, if everythin' holds, an' I can keep on livin' with jist one breath while I ought to be drawin' ten."

So it went in the soft, lazy night, the stranger and I following the battle without difficulty by the slow wakes of water.

Finally Dud said: "This is what Doc Brownin' used to call the momentous moment. Get my net, Mak. But keep back until I give the word. Then slip out in the river, about ten feet below me."

Dud's net is an institution, a commodious affair on the end of a stout ash stick, I have often seen strangers smile at that net. But it is Dud's net—built to fit his memories.

"Now I'm a-goin' to lead him in and let him run down to yer. When ye're sure he's in that net, sing out, becuz I want to let go the line. An' never mind what the books say about nettin' him tail on. You git his head down at the bottom, or he'll throw hisself out of it like a rat in a barrel."

The stranger handled the light. The big salmon came slowly down to me. I could see its dorsal fin cutting the water. At last I called out, and Dud slacked his line. Somehow I floundered ashore.

"Hold her up high," directed Dud.

"Good Lord!" said the stranger. "What a fish!"

"How much?" demanded Dud.

"How much! Why, name your own price."

"No, no. I mean, how much does he weigh?"

"Oh," said the stranger in a chastened tone. "Oh, twenty pounds."

"How much, Mak? Ye're holdin' the net."

"Between ten and twelve pounds."

"Hmp, he ain't half as big as I thought he was. But fer conversational purposes this young feller's estimate would be a goldanged sight smarter 'n yourn."

"By the Lord Harry!" shouted the stranger. "It has just come to me. You're Dud Dean himself!"

"Crotch, now that yer mention it, I believe I am."

"And didn't I hear you call this gentleman Mak?"

"Maybe so. I fergot to interduce you fellers."

"My name is Donald J. Bowen, sir."

"Well, Bowen, this is Macdougall."

"I seem to have been a jackass," said the stranger in a very sober voice.

Dud scratched his head and looked anxiously into the man's face. "Tell yer what. If ye'll accept it, I'd like to present this salmon to yer with Mak's an' my compliments. I was goin' to let the old cuss go back where he was born, but—"

Donald J. Bowen took the net out of my hands. "Gentlemen," he said "I accept this fish with the deepest gratitude. I'd like to have it mounted. It's my fish, is it?"

"Sartinly is," said Dud.

"All right. I'm crazy, but here goes!"

"Crotch!" gasped Dud in admiration.

I reached out a hand to hold the old warrior right side up. But at the touch of my fingers he righted himself and disappeared in the black waters beyond the rays of the light.

[41]

"Now why did I do that?" demanded Bowen in a subdued voice.

"So's ye'd have a good reason to come back an' fish the Kennebec next year," said Dud.

IV

CRAZY STILLER GOES A-FISHING

D UD DEAN and I were at Pierce Pond. Out in front were
the lisping waters, deeply inked with night shadows. On the
western sky line the black softwoods, blunt or spirelike, stood
against a faint wash of gray light. Over our heads were the
vaguely whispering spruce and pine, and over all, the stars. There
is, surely, something about the deep quiet of the wildlands that
awakens the soul. The artificialities of life slough off, and the
exacting rules of a man-made game are relegated to their own
insignificance.

"Is thar sunthin' in the Bible erbout a fool shall lead them?" Dud asked, breaking the spell.

I pulled myself back from vagrant meditations, and squinted at Dud. In the half-darkness I could just make out the lines of his face. He looked sober, but I suspected that there was a jocular vein in his question.

"Let's see," I mused, as though trying to recall something of the sort. "No, I don't remember anything just like that, but it sounds like one of the Proverbs. Doesn't it? Why?"

"Oh, nothin' much. I was jist thinkin' erbout how we come to find out that the biggest trout an' salmon, in our section of the woods, was in this lake."

"What do you mean? Haven't they always been here—the trout, I mean?"

"Now," said Dud, with a chuckle, "ye've raised what old Doc Brownin' w'ud call a controversial question. The answer is: Maybe so; then ag'in, maybe not. All I know is that nobudy ever dreamed thar was anythin' in this pond but pickerel, until erbout thirty-five years ago."

That was, to me, surprising information, since Pierce Pond is now famous for its nonmigratory salmon and big brook trout.

"Let's have the rest of the story," I suggested.

"Wel-el," drawled Dud, "I d'know's yer'd call it much of a story, but if yer don't mind a little hist'ry, I c'ud sort of help pass the evenin' off."

I nodded encouragingly. And Dud began his story.

Pierce Pond Stream is a hellion. She tumbles, from the old dam, almost straight down to the Kennebec River. This country had some mighty big punkin pine, not to mention such as spruce an' hemlock. So, erbout fifty years ago a bunch of lumbermen got together, an' built a dam at the outlet of this lake—what's left of that dam is down thar now. Then they started drivin' logs outer the lake—big logs that 'ud run a thousand feet to the tree, more er less.

I ain't a-doubtin' but that somebudy had fished here afore then, but that's erbout when the word went out that thar was nothin' in here but pickerel. Gosh! Some of them old-time pickerel w'ud remind yer of them pike we read erbout. Pickerel an' trout don't mix, as everybudy knows. The pickerel welcomes the trout 'ith wide-open mouths. An' bine-by the pickerel is lonely. I think that thar may have been, now an' then, a trout in Pierce Pond in them days, but they was certainly scarce. So folks sorta scratched this water off their fishin' list. In them days, it was considered low-down to fish fer sech common fish as pickerel. You can understand that. Nobudy is goin' to fool 'round 'ith pickerel as long as thar's more trout than a man can lug home.

Thar is a story—I've heard Dave Pooler tell it—that even the pickerel was planted in this lake. If it ain't true, God only knows how they got up here. Anyhow, 'bout the time they was lumberin' in here, a group of men that was addicted to fishin', as Nancy 'ud put it, took it inter their heads that they'd stock this big lake 'ith salmon, becuz it is a proven fact that once salmon git big enough to defend themselves, they hold their own ag'in all comers. 'N fact, it is contended that salmon'll drive the pickerel. Anyhow, only a few folks knew anythin' erbout the plans, since from time immemorial it has been the habit of fishermen to keep sech private enterprise to themselves. But them that did know was mostly of the mind that puttin' small salmon in this water w'udn't amount to no more'n a snowstorm on the last day of April. We figured that them salmon w'ud disappear like molasses an' pancakes in a lumber camp.

Now, consarnin' the actual plantin' of them fust Pierce Pond salmon, thar are five er six different stories, an' all of 'em are more er less apocryphal. Fer instance, it's claimed that the fust stockin' was western Quinnat salmon. I happened to be one of them that lugged them fust salmon up here, an' I know that they came from the Sebago Lake hatchery. They was what the fish experts call *Salmo salar sebago,* which is only to say that they was a sort of Atlantic salmon that ran up Sebago way, in the dim ages, an' fergot the way back to the sea. Our state fellers has been strippin' an' rearin' them fish fer a good many years. An' they was the best of all the nonmigratory salmon, by crotch.

Gen'rally speakin', thar has been four different sorts of salmon, all closely related to the Atlantic species, pretty carelessly planted in our ponds. Fust, the Federal Gover'ment has been raisin' Grand Lake nonmigratories. They've been at that erbout fifty years, I understand. An' as near's I've been able to study it out, them little salmon is practically the same as the now famous ouananiche of the St. John's waters. They never git mor'n five pounds heavy. Then the state ran some hatcheries at Green Lake, down in Washington County. Them Green Lake salmon uster run bigger'n the Schoodics did. In the third place, the regular sea-runners have been netted at the mouths of our rivers, an' stripped fer spawn. Yer'd s'pose that maybe them fish 'ud grow bigger than the nonmigratories in our inland lakes. But they don't.

As a matter of fact, thar ain't no salmon that ever matched our Sebago strain in fresh water. An' these Sebago is the fourth sort that yer'll find in our ponds. Now, as a matter of fact, it takes some studyin' to tell these salmon apart. I've guided some fish experts, in my day, an' that's how I come to know 'bout the situation. Size is erbout the only difference.

Long's I've got this far on a lecture, I might add that the western Quinnat has been put in a few of our Maine lakes. He grows like a house on fire, but so far has failed to establish hisself by spawnin', whereas the eastern fresh-water salmon will spawn successfully, if the inlets er outlets make it possible. Some years after we put the fust Sebago salmon in here, a few Quinnat salmon was planted. They grew wonderfully—thick an' pugnacious—but they never reached the weight of them Sebagos.

That jist erbout wades through all the yarns consarnin' the big fish of Pierce Pond. The various local yarns is true, but the truth is mixed up, as lies sometimes are, and as the best shift at the truth us poor human critters can muster often is.

Wel-el, I've sort of paddled up the wrong brook in this yarn, but I thought yer might be interested in the salmon puzzle. To git back, an' on with the yarn I had in mind, we dumped the fust can of little Sebagos in at the dam. An' it was no sooner done, than we see a dart of motion in the water, lookin' like a small submarine was comin'. How them poor little salmon did scatter! An' we see it warn't no use to dump any more in the pond proper; so we lugged the rest up two er three inlet streams, an' dumped 'em thar.

Erbout five years run along, an' all that time nobudy caught a dog-goned salmon. Those that had a hand in the plantin' of them fust fish did a lot of tryin', but we had to give up, an' admit that it certainly looked like the pickerel had cleaned them salmon, bones an' all. The spectators, them that was in on the know, all said, "We told yer so."

I guess it was only a year, er so, after that when a feller who went by the name of Crazy Stiller came to town. He was one of them knights of the sample case. I mean, he sold stuff, when he c'ud. He'd been comin' up this way fer two er three years, an' almost everybudy knew him well enough to call him by his popular nickname, which indicates better'n I can what he was like. Well, this time I'm gittin' at, he splashed inter town with a brand-new rod, an' a fishin' outfit good enough to make Hiram of Tyre turn green 'ith envy, as Doc Brownin' uster say.

"Where can I go to catch some real fish?" he asks Mark, who ran a general store.

Mark was usually on the alert to put a joke over. "C'ud yer stand a real hike, if yer was goin' to git some real fishin'?" he asks Crazy Stiller.

Crazy 'lowed that he c'ud climb the mountains of the moon to git some real big fish.

"Then," says Mark, with a wink at his store clerk, "if yer cross your heart, that yer won't tell, I'll tip yer off to a real place, where the biggest trout an' salmon in the universe is waitin' fer the ketchin'."

"Where is it?" says Crazy. "My gosh, man, don't think I'd ever tell a soul."

Of course, Jack Owens—that was the clerk's name—was won-derin' what Mark was comin' at. An' when Mark says, in an impressive whisper, "Pierce Pond," Jack got down under the backside of the counter, like he was after sunthin'. He told me afterward that he had to stick 'bout two yards of towelin' into his mouth. "Pierce Pond!" thinks Jack. "That's rich! Nothin' but a pickerel pond at the end of a three-mile climb up a mountain."

But Crazy Stiller was green at fishin', an' greener'n that erbout the country 'round here, so he swallowed all the bunk Mark handed him.

"I've got to git me a guide," he says. "Who'd yer recommend?"

Wel-el, Crazy's thinkin' that he needed a guide was how I come into the pitchur. Mark called me in. Crazy was hoverin' around, an' Mark purty near had a fit, tryin' to wise me up. Finally I got the idea. An' I agreed to go. I have never regretted it.

Before we left, on the Caratunk stage, 'bout half of the fellers in town was wise, an' so many of them come 'round to wish us luck that it seemed to me the cat w'ud fall through the bottom of the bag. But Crazy jist got all preened up, an' it never entered his head that erbout everybudy seemed to know all 'bout Mark's secret.

At Caratunk the Kennebec was high, an' we dum near upset the canoe, gittin' across. I must say that Crazy s'prised me some, when we started up the mountain to Pierce Pond. In them days thar warn't even so much of a trail as thar is now. In places yer had to hang on with your teeth, as yer might say. I was luggin' most everythin', but his new rod, which he w'udn't trust to me. He was as excited as a kid goin' to his fust circus, an' finally he 'lowed that he'd go on ahead. Not bein' excited, myself, I let him go it, an' took my own time. So, 'cordin' to his tell, he got to the pond a half hour b'fore I did.

Anyway, when I got thar, I see him a-runnin' up an' down the shore by the dam, an' it was plain to see he was all worked up. When he see me, he waved his rod an' yelled, "I've seen four jump already. Git that tackle box open." Crotch, he was all pantin' and wheezy 'ith excitement.

So I opens up his little tin trunk, an' thar was the gol-darnedest mess of stuff yer ever see.

"What'll I try fust?" he wanted to know.

I said that I guessed it didn't make much difference.

"That's right," he says. "They'll take anything."

It was my opinion that pickerel w'udn't take flies, though I know now that ain't true, an' so I hitched on a small copper spoon, 'ith a little silver tip on it.

Crazy! Gosh, if ever a nickname fitted, it was his'n. When I'd got his riggin' ready, he fetched his castin' rod three er four times 'round his head; give a gosh awful heave; an' let her go in the general direction of the pond. Away went the spoon an' line, like a bullet. But the spoon went faster'n the line, an' fetched up away out in the pond. An' by crotch, it no sooner hit the water than, *whang!* Judgin' from the commotion out thar, yer'd have said that the spoon exploded. I had been settin' down, but yer can bet I got up, an' stared at the place where that piece of junk had struck.

"Did yer see that?" shouts Crazy. "Didjer see that fish?"

His questions kinda took me off guard, an' I says, "Crotch, but that must have been a big pickerel!"

"Pickerel!" says Crazy Stiller, kinda scornful an' superior.

"Pickerel? Say, I'm beginnin' to think that Mark Savage has put sunthin' over on me."

Bein' honest at heart, I nodded. But that warn't what he meant becuz he went on to say:

"Sendin' me off with a guide that don't know a pickerel from a salmon when he sees it. Here, give me another one of them shiny spoons. An' this time see that yer tie it on so it'll stay."

I pawed 'round in that tin casket of his'n, but nothin' like the spoon he'd lost had been buried in it. So I hitched up a tin fish, all painted like one of them war transports. Crazy fetched three er four more circles 'round his head, an' I ducked fer cover. Honest, he knew so blamed little 'bout fishin' that he c'udn't have thrown an anchor overboard. But finally he let her go at the pond. That tin sucker went erbout six feet, an' he had one beaut of a backlash.

"Here," he says, "you unfix this, an' I'll try the other rod."

But before he had begun on his new fly rod, an' idea stung him, an' he jumped an' shouts, "I've got an idea." An' away he races fer the woods.

I went to unsnarlin' his castin' line, but it warn't more'n a min-it, when back he come, with a big nightwalker squirmin' an' wigglin' between his fingers. Usually, you know, a feller can't find a worm in the woods—not a regular angleworm, I mean— but he had happened on a place where somebudy had dumped some, one time er another. Speakin' of luck, that feller was her adopted son.

Naturally, I didn't pay much attention to him, bein' as I was busy unsnarlin' his last idea, but I see him strugglin' to git that worm on a big hook. Bine-by, he heaves it out, with erbout a pound of lead, to make sure it w'udn't float, I s'pose. An' then was when I got the surprise of my life. Fer that bait no sooner hit the water than he got the dum-dest strike yer ever see. I tell yer that I fergot all erbout that backlash, an' tried to take his fly rod away from him.

"Let go of that!" he screams. "Let go, I tell yer!"

Thar was a kind of a wild light in his eyes, so I set down ag'in. No pickerel is worth fightin' over, an' I s'posed that was what he had hooked. But after pullin' an' pullin', an' it was nip an' tuck which w'ud bust the rod fust, by crotch if he didn't land the purtiest trout I ever laid my eyes on. Of course he busted his tip all to pieces.

"Get your net," he shouts at me.

"Net?" I says. "You mean a baseball bat."

I'm not lyin'. That same trout weighed nine pounds an' fourteen ounces, which is the biggest brook trout I ever see. My gosh! My gosh! An' that nitwit caught him with a nightwalker!

After that, we hunted fer more worms. But the one Crazy found must have been the last of his race. When he—I mean Crazy, not the worm—was convinced that thar warn't no more worms ter be had, he let me rig up a cast of flies. As a matter of fact, he had bought a sample of every fly that was invented, an' some that was never invented, but was jist born of delirium tremors an' plumb foolishness.

The way that dub cast them flies was e-nough to make Napoleon cry like an old maid. I had to hold on to a tree to keep from hittin' him. But believe me er not, the fourth splash he made, I see a big streak of silver, like a stick of pulpwood in size, hit his fly. *Bang!* An' that was all.

[52]

"He's gone," sobs the big slob. "He's g-g-g-one!"

"So's your leader," I says.

Wel-el, I hitched up another leader. An' it was the same story over ag'in. *Whang! Bang!* Then he managed to hook a good one, an' broke the second tip. But he had one left. An' after some bunglin', he managed to cast out another fly. Up come another salmon, like a jack-in-the-box. When that fish began to ask fer more line, Crazy Stiller jist hung back all the harder. His eyes bunged out, like one of them dolls that says "Mamma" when yer turn it upside down.

I was half luny myself by that time, "By crotch," I says, "let that fish go!" Up flopped the salmon ag'in. "Let him go!" I hollers. "Give him line! Ease up on him, yer durn idgit. Let him go! D'yer hear me?"

"Let him go!" says the big tub of lard. "Let him go? Why should I let him go? I want him."

By crotch, I was so plumb beside myself that I was standin' on one leg, like a pie-eyed crane. "You crotchly lunkhead," I shouts at him, "if yer don't give that fish some line, I'll murder yer."

But it warn't no use. Jist then that salmon give a leap bigger an' better'n any hitherto, an' he was gone. Crazy started bawlin' like a two-year-old. "He's, he's gone, too," he blubbers.

"Give me that rod," I says, grabbin' it from him. Then I took a cast, guessin' that it warn't no use, after all that commotion. But so help me Hannibal, as Doc Brownin' uster say, if I didn't git a strike that knocked the reel loose—anyway it dropped off inter the lake. That fish got plenty of line, all right. An' of course he run with it, an' didn't show hisself. Finally, I got that

[53]

reel back on, an' snubbed the old cuss. He went up in the air like a rocket. He kinda seemed to shake hisself all over, but I'd got a good tight line by that time. *Whish*, he goes; then up he goes. Down deep, he goes, like his watch had dropped out of his pocket, an' gone to the bottom. I had to lift on him some, becuz it ain't safe, ever, to let one of them old stagers go cruisin' around on the bottom. An' up he comes, like he'd found the watch, an' was goin' to hang it on a Christmas tree.

Gosh! No wonder I keep a-fishin', an' a-dreamin' to do that all over ag'in. Crazy had a good rod. Sometimes I was out in the pond, up to my belt, er more. Sometimes I was runnin' up an' down the shore, an' at sech times, Crazy kept gittin' in my way; shoutin' directions at me; an' tryin' to take his rod away from me. I got so mad I warn't a gentleman no longer. Next thing I knew he had fell down right in front of where I was goin'. Of course, I fell on top of him. He sorta groaned, but I was so mad, when I got up ag'in, that I give him a kick where he'd mind it least. But I didn't have no time to stop an' see what effects the kick had on him, 'cause that fish was a-jumpin' ag'in.

We was goin' through that sort of thing fer a good, long hour, but in spite of Crazy, an' everythin' else, I tuckered that fish. He was an old male, with his under jaw curled up over his nose. He was the best landlocked salmon I ever see, an' he weighed twenty-two pounds, not to mention some odd ounces.

Wel-el, Crazy went at it ag'in, down nearer the dam, an' he got strikes enough to bust up the rest of his riggin'. So we struck out fer home. By that time, I had cooled off some, so I let Crazy have the salmon to go 'ith his nice squaretail. When we got down to Caratunk, he told, right in front of me, that he caught that big salmon on an angleworm, same's he did the trout.

"Ye've heard of the gold rush of '49," said Dud, winding up his tale. "Well, that's jist the way it was around here, an' it ain't all over yit. When we got to Bingham, Crazy showed his fish all over town. Of course yer never saw sech a foolish lookin' bunch as them fellers was that had spoofed him inter goin' to Pierce Pond. They was all set to kid the pants off'n him, so they was all flabbergasted when he showed up with them big fish.

"Yep, it started an exodus to Pierce Pond. Oh, well," concluded Dud, knocking the ashes out of his pipe, "if thar ain't sunthin' in the Bible erbout a fool shall lead them, thar sh'ud be."

V

ONCE IN THE STILLY NIGHT

D UD DEAN held the empty frying pan over the coals of
our little fire. The fat caught, flared and burned out. After that
burst of yellow light, the night seemed darker, blacker than
before.

"Trout are middlin' fodder," said Dud, as he laid aside the
pan and drew his pipe from his shirt pocket.

There was nothing to add to that; so I settled back against a
beech tree and stretched my legs toward the little fire. Dud
paused in the act of pouring a palmful of cut plug into the bowl

of his pipe. We heard a distinct sniffing a few feet beyond the campfire's fringe of light.

"Porcupine," I guessed aloud.

In a moment I secured a flashlight from the pack at my side. And the light caught a half-grown raccoon sniffing at the fish bones we had lately thrown aside.

Dud chuckled. "Cunnin' little cuss. And that reminds me, all of a sudden, of the time I went rarecoon huntin'."

"Coon hunting?"

"Aya. Thar's a sport we've neglected up this way, although coons ain't what yer'd call thick. Up to the time I was persuaded to enlist, I had occasionally read erbout it, but had never participated. It was a feller by the name of Shurtliff, who lived down to Lewiston, that talked me into goin'. He sold pickles, but mostly I guess that he talked hounds an' rarecoons. He claimed that he sold fifty-seven sorts of pickles, an' had owned fifty-eight coon hounds, and that his last was the champion of the lot. This last hound's name was Vinegar.

"Shurtliff was interduced to me downtown. 'Well, well,' he says, 'so ye're Dud Dean? I've heard that yer know more erbout trout than Izaak Walton, hisself, but what do yer know about coon hounds?'

" 'I can tell 'em from Pointers,' I says.

" 'I sh'ud hope so!' he says. 'How w'ud yer like to go rarecoon huntin' with me, some night?'

"Wel-el, it really didn't appeal to me, but I c'udn't put that feller off. So in due time I went. And it turned out to be the most crotchly night I ever put in o'er land er sea. If that was a sample of coon huntin', a feller has to take events jist as they come, an' nobudy is so much subjected to the caprice an' damp humor of circumstances as the coon hunter is apt to be. Still, it's a grand sport, if yer can take it.

"Shurtliff brung two other fellers from his town. One was named Joseph and the other Louis. But Shurtliff talked, mostly, erbout his dog. Accordin' to his talk, an ordinary coon hound sometimes strayed from the straight and narrow path, but not Vinegar. Vinegar never chased anythin' but coons.

"I'm afraid that put an idea in my head. I really didn't know where to look for rarecoons, but I felt purty sure I c'ud find Vinegar a skunk. An' it kinda tickled my perversity to think erbout sech an adventure. Y'see, back in the summer I had been 'tendin' to some fishin' down on the Old Lake Road. On my way out, I had to haul up, while a she-skunk as big as Rhode Island sort of sauntered across the road. She was proudly followed by six duplicates in smaller calibers. That made seven, as I thought it over, an' it didn't seem too farfetched to imagine that thar was one more in the neighborhood. That made eight. So I suggested that we try the rarecoon huntin' erlong the Old Lake Road.

"It was a purty night, when we started out. The moon was as big as an Irishman's heart, an' the road over Babbit Ridge was as plain as day. When we reached the fields around the Ben Adams Place, everythin' looked mighty purty in the silver light.

" 'Let's leave the car here,' I suggested, when we came to the four corners. 'Maybe we'll pick up a coon track while we're walkin' up the old road.'

" 'Are they that thick?' says Joseph.

" 'Thicker,' I says, thinkin' of them skunks.

"But b'crotch, that Vinegar acted like he was one dog that was purty near as good as his owner claimed. If he winded any skunks, he never paid any attention. Fust, he got out of the car, tail in the air, an' sniffed and snuffed. Next he galloped off, like he'd got the situation in hand. We hustled to git all our trappings tergether. It seems that yer always want to take all yer can lug on a coon hunt; becuz the more yer start with, the less ye'll git back 'ith.

"Shurtliff an' Joe took the lanterns. Louis pulled out a little rifle that he declared had an ivory bead on it which c'ud be seen in the dark. Well, he sure needed it before that night was done. The moon got off her trail and never got back on it. The sky got black as the inside of a felt hat, an' a damp wind begun to blow from the south.

" 'Listen,' I says to Shurtliff, when we'd gone erbout ten rods.

"All hands stopped and listened. Lo an' b'hold, Vinegar was jist a-tearin' pages out of his music book—rip, rippity, rip. An' whatever it was that he was chasin', it was headed 'bout easterly, opposite the little white schoolhouse.

" 'That's him,' says Shurtliff.

"I c'ud have told him that the verb 'to be' never takes an object, as I've heard Nancy say more'n a thousand times, but what is the use of a feller talkin' what he don't believe hisself? I let it pass. What was puzzlin' me was how we was ever goin' to git to that rarecoon, if that Vinegar hound kept on chasin' him out of the country.

"At fust, we didn't hurry any to speak of, but bineby that dog begun to bark tree. By that time, we was jist opposite the Vigue Place, and Shurtliff an' Joe jist left me an' Louis. I was lank an' fit in them days, but those two fellers had been trained in a sport that turns out supermen in the legs. They lit out like the devil had 'em by the tail, an' was twistin' it at every jump. Of course, they had the lanterns which was some advantage. Louis an' me w'ud have made better time, if we had been able to see where we was going.

"As it was, I kept busy tryin' to keep up with Louis, whose feet was faster'n his jedgment. The fust thing I really see, after we left the road, was a big pine tree right in front of me. I thought it looked sort of familiar, but when ye're all out of wind, even old acquaintance is apt to be fergot. I see that Louis had dodged the pine, but in a few steps he fetched up ag'in sunthin' else. It laid him out, flat, like he'd been punched in the chin. Up he got an' ducked to the left. An' down he went ag'in. That time, he lay where he'd fallen.

" 'Where am I?' he says to me, when I helped him to get to his feet.

" 'Ye're in a graveyard,' I says. 'Ye've run plum down the middle of it, and fetched up ag'in the back fence.'

"Yer see, the old front gate had been wide open, an' since it was built plenty wide we got in all easy, but the way out warn't so easy, which is typical of sech places.

"After Louis got his wind, he was satisfied to let me lead the way. When we got to the spot where Vinegar was barkin,' I see that he'd apparently run his game up a thunderin' big basswood. Fust, he'd put his paws up as far as he c'ud reach, an' then throw back his head, an' let her roll. Then he'd go around the tree an' repeat. Joe had broken his lantern, an' was riggin' up a little carbide light, which he had had all the time. It looked like them guys either thought me an' Louis c'ud see in the dark, er didn't care a dang.

"As near as I c'ud make out this was a big occasion. I certainly admired Vinegar's voice. The yowls run out of him like buckshot out of a tin horn. Bineby, Joe got so he c'ud train his light on the tree. It was as empty of rarecoons as a prayer meetin' is. of hoss traders. But one of them basswoods is sure to be as hollow as a blue heron; so we looked the old tree over. It was perfectly plain that a man c'udn't climb a tree like that, not even if Paul Bunyan hisself had been thar to boost him.

" 'Well, thar's jist one thing to do,' says Shurtliff, 'an' that is to smoke 'em out.'

" 'But thar hain't no hole to build a fire in,' says Joe.

" 'If we had only brought erlong an ax,' says Louis, 'we c'ud chop a hole.'

" 'Yes,' says Shurtliff, kinda scornful, 'if we had an ax, we c'ud cut this durned tree down flat.'

"I must say that it looked like a purty pickle, as Shurtliff w'ud have said hisself in a more rational moment. But Vinegar solved the problem by racin' off to another tree. In erbout two jerks of a buck's tail, he was barkin' up, like the basswood had been a sorry mistake. To this day, I d'know whether he had made an error, er but that the woods was full of rarecoons. Of course, Shurtliff an' his pal, Joe, left everythin'—but the lantern. However it was a short go, an' me an' Louis warn't far behind at the finish. That time, Vinegar had picked out a rock maple. Joe's light found a pair of eyes that was lookin' down on us like they hated the sight of us. Shurtliff insisted that he had better do the shootin', but Louis was stubborn an' w'udn't give in.

"If Louis got that ivory bead on that coon, he must have aimed at the wrong end of the critter. That was my fust experience 'ith a peeved coon. When it lit in our midst, it was fightin' mad. I took a kick at it with the toe of my right boot, but missed, an' hit Vinegar in the jaws. Crotch, but warn't I ashamed of myself. Vinegar let a bellow out of him, like it didn't feel none too good, but seemed to think that the coon had done it.

"For a little while it looked to me like that rarecoon was goin' to be too much fer Vinegar, but at last the old hound got a grip on the coon, an' never let go. I felt kinda sorry. It's too bad when a good fight has to end that way. I always like to see it a draw.

"Vinegar hadn't a mite of int'rest in a dead coon. Jist went off inter the night, an' left it with us to skin-out number one. Joe produced a business-like knife. 'Number one,' says Shurtliff, with jist as much satisfaction as though he'd licked the coon hisself. It was a good chance fer me to git the lantern, an' I laid hold on it, in case Vinegar sh'ud find some more coons. It warn't more'n three min-its, until I knew I'd done a smart thing. Ag'in, Vinegar begun to bellow as loud as it was dark. Shurtliff jist dove off with the other light, an' we left Joe a-skinnin' his coon in the dark.

"That time, I was ahead all of the way, until I busted out in a little piece of pasture, an' dang-near ran inter proof a-plenty that I was in the vanguard. By crotch if thar warn't the same she-skunk I'd seen in the summer, it was her spittin' image. She looked as big as a dead hoss, to me, an' I put on the breaks so fast that yer c'ud have heard me skid in the wet grass. While I stood thar, on the fringe of things, Shurtliff and Louis went by me like the wind on a pond. Purty soon thar was a mighty thrashin' in the brush, an' out came Joe, a-wavin' that skinnin' knife in his right hand. But he warn't the least mad. 'This place,' he sings out at me, 'must be full of coons.' Of course none of 'em paid any attention to me. If they had, they'd have heard what I said, becuz I didn't whisper it. If the place was full of rarecoons, thar was an almighty skunk wedged in between.

"When them fellers from Lewiston had taken in the situation, we all gathered round with considerable caution. Vinegar did a lot of growlin' and threatenin' but kept it in mind that he weren't dealin' with no coon. While we was considerin', Louis stepped forward, an' said that he was goin' to shoot her head off. I backed up, some more. But Shurtliff jist waved Louis to the rear, like he was David bein' offered Saul's armor.

" 'I'll pick her up by the tail,' he says. 'They can't atomize, when their feet is off the ground.'

" 'Then what'll yer do,' demands Louis.

" 'Then you crack her in the head with a club, an' thar won't be any mess at all.'

" 'A skunk like that hain't worth the risk,' says Louis.

" 'Every last one of them critters sh'ud be exterminated,' says Shurtliff, glaring at the old girl, who had her head in a little pile of rocks, but her battery facin' the foe. 'We have got to do it in the int'rest of sport, but thar ain't no sense in stirrin' up a cyclone. It can be done neatly and with dispatch. If yer was to shoot at her, like enough ye'd jist nick her.'

" 'Is that so!' says Louis. 'Well, I'd rather have a nicked skunk in the bush than a live one in my hands.'

"Nobudy laughed at that. Finally Joe says, 'I'll crack her, if

[66]

ye'll hold her, high an' dry.' So Shurtliff told Vinegar to go in an' get at her—the idea bein' to take the skunk's mind off'n him an' Joe. But shucks, a skunk ain't got a mind. Old Vinegar knew that, an' walked stiff-legged around his victim. But when she warn't lookin'. Shurtliff walked in on tiptoe, an' jerked her free an' clear at arm's length. I must say that he struck me like a man 'ith more courage than precaution. But by crotch nothin' happened. Even Vinegar acted like he c'uldn't believe his eyes er nose.

"Joe walked in 'ith his stick.

" "Steady, now,' says Shurtliff.

" 'All set?' says Joe.

" 'Let her have it,' says Shurtliff, purty tight lipped.

"I guess that skunk thought Shurtliff was talkin' to her, becuz she let them have it!

"Shurtliff dropped the critter. Vinegar got so excited that he rushed in an' grappled with her. I'd have laughed, if it had choked me. An' it durn near did.

"Vinegar finished the skunk, without assistance. An' all I c'ud think of as we went along out of thar was the line erbout a vase in which roses has once been distilled—how if yer break an' shatter it, the scent of the roses remains 'ith it still. But by the time we come out to the road ag'in, Shurtliff's spirits had so far revived that he c'ud whistle, 'Thar'll be a hot time in the old town tonight.' I don't think that anythin' ever kept him down, fer long. The world was his brine, as yer might say.

"We left Vinegar behind. When I see him last, he was plowin' his nose through the grass, an' foamin' at the mouth. But he an' Shurtliff was erbout alike, as a dog an' master sh'ud be, an' when we stepped inter the road, Vinegar bounded out after us, like nothin' at all had happened, but *not* smellin' that way. Louis said that we might's well go home, becuz the hound wu'dn't be able to smell anythin' fer a week, which didn't sound probable to me.

" 'Cheer up,' says Joe, 'we've got one—Say! where is that coon!'

"That was one of them rhetorical questions, becuz he knew durn well that he'd left that coon right where we left him skinnin' it.

" 'Well,' says Louis purty disgusted, 'I must say that this is a damned fine beginnin'.'

"Up to the old Brown place thar's an old side road to the west that leads off to some more old, fergotten farms. We took that. In places it was full of alders, which ain't the easiest things to git through in the dark. But we had to take it becuz Vinegar was barkin' in thar. Shurtliff got his shoe caught in the crotch of an alder, and fell on his face. He talked sunthin' fierce, but it didn't have any effect on the alders. To help matters out, Joe had to fall down, too, an' the lantern he was carryin' went out. But we lit her up ag'in, an' went on. Thar's that eternal principle erbout coon huntin'—to go on, an' let the dead bury their dead.

"Finally, from away up on top the hill, we heard Vinegar announcin' to the tall night that he'd treed his game. Gittin' to a dog that's barkin' up ain't so much of a picnic as yer'd suppose. Every bush an' branch in the woods reaches out an' takes a hunk out of your clothes, an' now an' then, ye'll lose a patch of hide. The woods don't seem friendly in the dark.

"When we did reach Vinegar, he set up a tarnation of a noise, around a birch as big as a barrel, an' taller'n a tree ought to be. When we got the carbide light on the object of our chase, it was plain that Vinegar hadn't made no mistake this time. But the eyes that glared back at us looked shifty an' too far apart to me. Louis drew a bead on 'em, that was as careless as a kid shootin' a robin.

"'Hold on,' I says, 'sunthin' tells me that it 'ud be a mistake to hit that critter where yer hit that coon. I had a whole lot rather have Shurtliff pick it up by the tail.'

"'Aw, hurry up,' says Shurtliff, lookin' scornful at me, 'we hain't got all night to spend in this place.'

"It looked like Louis did hurry up, becuz I don't believe he even nicked that bobcat. It slid out of the tree, from the back side, like a chap 'ith skis on his feet. Nobudy ever called Dud Dean a coward—twice—an' I rushed around with the rest of 'em. Vinegar muckled that bobcat, right where he lit on the ground. Fer a moment, it was quite a fight. I got too close one spell, an' if that cat didn't make a pass at me, I was in a high state of excitement. 'Bout then, the cat walloped Vinegar so hard that he let a howl out of him a yard long. Joe had to drop the lantern, an' of course the danged thing went out ag'in, which left it fifty per cent darker.

"All through it, Vinegar displayed more courage than jedgment. Him an' the bobcat was jist a confusion. Louis hopped around with his gun pointed fust at the hound and then at the cat. Finally, I yanked the weapon out of his hands. But by that time the bobcat was gone, like the night had reached out an' taken him off. Even Vinegar c'udn't believe it fer as much as twenty seconds. When he did, he raced off like the soldier he was. An' we all took after the noise Vinegar was makin'; but crotch, we never did catch up 'ith them ag'in. They treed four or five times, but the durn cat w'udn't stay treed. It was tarnation goin'. I believe that we actually went through growths of young firs that the wind c'udn't have blown through. All in all, we was up an' down—tripped down, knocked down, an' jist plain down, causes unaccounted fer—more than a hundred times.

"Bineby I begun to wonder where we was, anyway. But Shurtliff didn't seem to think that was at all important. He seemed to think that as long as we followed that bobcat we'd come out on the main street of Lewiston in the end. But I had begun to feel sure that we was as good as lost—turned 'round—right then. Finally I said so. Say, them fellers was scornful. Even Louis was indignant, an' declared that he had never been lost in his life. Meantime, Vinegar had gone out of hearin'.

"So I give it up. I knew an awful good cure fer what ailed them rarecoon hunters, an' decided to let it work. I let them have their own way. Gosh, it was fun! We tramped 'round and 'round, like little children playin' ring around the rosy—only thar warn't no rosy, jist us hunters lost out in the Almighty's black night. At least, I was sure that I didn't have no more idea where I was than Larb Blare had the time he got pifficated, an' wandered into the Methodist church.

"Bineby, danged if we didn't cross a road with thick alders in it. Thinks I, 'Shurtliff will recognize this place.' But he didn't. So we circled 'round some more, until we crossed that road ag'in. I had to laugh out loud—struck me that way, yer know.

"'What yer laughin' at?' says Shurtliff in a provoked voice.

"I never bothered to answer him. A man don't need to answer sech questions in the long run. Finally, we struck off ag'in, but didn't come back to the road no more. After Shurtliff had fallen over the same windfall a half dozen times in half an hour, he admitted that the woods was full of blowdowns. I sat down. I was tired, tired as a dog on the Fourth of July.

" 'What's the matter?' says Shurtliff, sort of teeterin' on his feet.

" 'Nothin',' I says, 'except that I'm kinda dizzy.'

"It was Joe's turn, so he seemed to think. 'Ye're damned right,' he says, 'condemn it! We've been travelin' in a circle fer the last ten min-its. Now what'll we do?'

" 'Well,' I says, 'I've always heard that the thing to do, when ye're lost, is to sit down, an' act calm. If that don't appeal to you fellers, we can keep on followin' Shurtliff, until he drops dead.'

"Somehow, I guess Shurtliff didn't like that, but of course he'd known fer a long time that he didn't know where he was. So we sot. It was still in them woods. And it was as dark as underground. It made a man feel unimportant without anybudy's help. Nobudy said anythin'. I watched our lantern burnin' low, and when it sputtered out, it struck me that it was a little tin symbol of all man's efforts to git along in the Almighty's night of all time. 'Long erbout that time, I fell to thinkin' how good my own bed 'ud feel, if I was in it. I tried to think of sunthin' that was softer than a feather bed, but I c'udn't. 'Bout then, I 'spose, I went to sleep.

"When I woke up, it was rainin' a little. The other rarecoon hunters was sleepin'. It's kinda funny to watch the rain fall on a face that don't know it. When I got up an' looked around, I swear that I c'udn't see nothin' that looked familiar. But I seen a stunpile, which indicated that we was in some grown-up farmin' land.

"In a min-it Joe woke up. He got to his feet; an' looked about in considerable bewilderment. Then he says, 'What's that back-end of a little white buildin' over thar?'

"I looked over where he was p'intin', an' I was some surprised myself. 'That,' I says, like I'd known it all the time, 'is the little old schoolhouse we come by last night.'

"By crotch, if we hadn't put in the tag end of the night, after Vinegar had gone out of hearin', wanderin' eround an' finally sleepin' within a few rods of Shurtliff's car. Joe woke up the other two in a hurry, an' we legged it fer the automobile. When we got to it, thar was Vinegar, curled up in the back seat. An' the scent of the roses hung 'round him still."

VI

MEN AND MICE

FOR hours Dud Dean and I had been trying one fly after another. And all that time erratic gusts of wind had been blowing across the upper pond, dying out, mournfully, in the pines along the wild and ragged shores. It seemed to me that, as far back as I could remember, cold rain water had been running down my trouser legs and into my boots.

Dud squinted at me through a maze of pipe smoke and chuckled.

"The general aspect," he said, "reminds me of Hannah Bealey.

She was remarried so many times that the town clerk lost track of the record. An' thar warn't a single one of her men that was the sort to bring home in broad daylight. Somebody asked her if she felt as nervous an' excited the last time as she'd been the fust. 'Well,' she says, 'maybe I was as nervous, but I warn't so expectant.'

"To tell the bare-naked truth, I've kinda lost my expectancy this afternoon; but shucks, a body c'udn't apply that to fishin' in general. It takes more'n a cold an' wet behind to permanently discourage a fisherman. When I git sot down in that rocker of mine, pulled up to the fire, I'll no more be able to remember this weather than the second generation of Israelites c'ud remember makin' bricks out of straw."

"Bricks without straw," I suggested.

At that, another cranky gust of wind blew patterns of rain helter-skelter across upper Pierce Pond. The chill of it seemed to lay hold of every muscle in my body with fingers as cold as January. And a violent shiver ran, like a varying hare, crisscross, back and forth, and up and down my plagued person. That shiver actually sent a tremor along the boat.

Dud looked up from a sober study of his open fly book.

"Say, Mak, I've noticed that whenever yer write one of them fishin' stories of yourn the weather is as nice and balmy as a mornin' in Beulah Land. If it's mornin', up comes the sun, not too bright, but warm. If it's at the middle of the day, it may look like rain, but it never does. An' by gosh, ye're a past master at sunsets an' twilights. Everything is always warm an' purty. Maybe thar's a wind, but it don't make no more disturbance on the water 'n a fisherman's ripple.

"The woods is apt to be full of singin' birds; the sky is full of colors, dyin'; nine times out of ten, the May flies, or sunthin', hatch all over the place, an' the water is full of trout. If a body stops to think it over, he suspects that yer must have some sort of super weather service, an' that your old red shirt ain't never been rained on.

"Why don't yer write the next story out in a leaky woodshed, with your feet in a tub of water? Then, as like as not, yer c'ud write a story of a trip like this 'un in sech a way that everybody that read it w'ud reach fer a raincoat."

The good Lord knows that I love Dud Dean, as Jonathan loved David, but somehow that piece of advice did not please me. My eyes wandered off across the weary reaches of water, rolling before the wind. One old pine, a veteran of a hundred years or more, was half lost from sight in a drift of the wettest and most melancholy fog I had ever seen.

"This," I replied, "isn't a fishing trip. It's an ordeal. No one would care to read about a fishing trip like this."

Dud chuckled, his head bent over the fly book, in which he sought a fly that would coax up a trout where none had appeared to previous offerings. That chuckle seemed to me to be a triumph of spirit over matter. Somewhat inspired, or shamed, I decided that some topic for good conversation would fill in the time, until Dud himself might suggest that we go home. Since Dud had but lately touched upon fishing stories, I decided that topic would do. And that perennially delightful story of John Taintor Foote's came to mind.

"The best fishing yarn I ever read," I said, "was 'The Wedding Gift.'"

Perhaps that was introducing my project too abruptly, for Dud looked up, his forehead still puckered from concentration over his book of wet-fly patterns, and said, "Crotch, are yer kinda wet under your hat?"

I explained that my idea had been to start a conversation to pass the time away, and asked, "Did you ever read 'The Wedding Gift'?"

"Sartinly, I've read it. We've got it to home—printed in a nice little book a feller sent Nancy one Christmas. He writ on the front page, 'Fer the lady who can make the best doughnuts in all the world.' Nancy was all set up over it. Don't it beat all how human folks are? Well, it's a good yarn, middlin' good."

"Why, it's a classic," I said, warming about the heart.

"Aya. Did I ever tell yer about the preacher that sort of overstepped hisself, Mak?"

"No," I admitted, wondering just what Dud was leading toward.

"Didn't I ever tell yer that yarn? Ain't that a sight! Nancy an' me was tourin' up in Aroostuck County. An' we went in to a camp-meetin' of the Holier than Thou. A few of the Holier than Them had sort of elbowed in. The preacher was a powerful feller. When he got warmed up, he put me in mind of a windmill. An' by an' by he got out of control an' burned out his brake linings. He was contendin' that sunthin' or other was the only passport to heaven, an' wound up shoutin' that the other crowd had neglected to preach that doctrine. 'I'll bet a hundred dollars,' he says, 'that they ain't got a preacher in their crowd that preaches it.'

"That created a sensation, becuz in them days it was con-

sidered scandalous to so much as bet a cigar. Ye c'ud have heard
a dollar bill drop in the collection basket, it was so still. The
preacher hisself was awful took back at his own words, I guess.
An' if the Almighty warn't shocked, Nancy was. If Queen
Victoria had spit on the floor, Nancy c'udn't have been no more
upset.

"About then a tall feller, that was split up to his collarbone,
got to his feet an' cleared his throat, like a buck deer that's
winded sunthin,' I recognized him, becuz he'd gone up an' down
the state of Maine preachin' to beat the devil, as Doc Brownin'
used to say. He was considered the leadin' preacher fer the
opposition. Wel-el, folks jist sucked in their breath an' sagged
back in their seats. It looked like the devil hisself had delivered
that preacher into that tall feller's hands. But I guess the tall
feller had been kinda carried away by the other feller's passion,
an' what he seemed to have in mind was to show up the fact
that this preacher didn't have no hundred dollars to back up his
talk. Anyhow, he cleared his throat ag'in, like Naaman by the
Jordan River, an' in a thundering voice said, 'Mister Preacher,
when you said that ye'd bet a hundred dollars that none of us
preached that doctrine, did yer mean it, or was yer just
preachin'?'

"Point I'm comin' at is that if yer really mean that this or
that is the best fishin' story I want to rise up an' say that the
best story I ever read was 'The Spickle Fisherman,' which was
writ by a feller whose name is White."

"Never read it," I confessed.

"Spickle fish is trout in our talk. Only this was a tormented big
trout. Yes, sir! Lived in one of those streams that's hired out and

has a clubhouse on its banks. It was a dry-fly club. Most of its members w'udn't have known an angleworm if they had seen it in the movin' pitchurs. 'Long comes an old feller that was sort of a relative to King Solomon. He'd never done any fishin'. He'd jist spent a lot of time wantin' to go fishin'.

"It was an awful big trout, Mak, a crotchly big trout, an' they'd all been tryin' to take it. In fact, I jedge that trout had kept up their membership fer several years. As I remember it, the old feller didn't have no right to fish in that stream, let alone with a can full of worms. One day he met one of the members an' asked him what he s'posed a man needed fer bait to catch that big trout, an' in a moment of fine scorn, sech as us fly fishermen is apt to nurse, he says, 'Oh, he'd prob'ly take a live mouse.' So, by crotch, the old feller got him some mice—micers, he called 'em—an' he caught that trout! Of course, thar's more to the story than that."

"That reminds me," I said, "of something I saw happen at Lost Pond a few nights ago. It was just about sunset—maybe a little the west side of sunset. I was out on a raft, and was casting inshore. A deer mouse ran out on a dead stick that hung over the water. When it came to the end of the stub, it either jumped in of its own volition, or it fell off. Anyway, a big trout nailed it, quicker than a weasel."

"And?" prompted Dud.

"And the old cuss wouldn't come to a fly."

"Had his belly full of micers, most likely."

"And," I continued, "Dave Pooler told me about opening up a big trout he caught in Lindsey Cove. It had a full-grown mouse in its stomach."

"But it w'udn't be much like fishin' to use mice," observed Dud.

"Certainly it would not," I agreed. "Besides, we haven't got any mice."

Dud looked up into the leaden sky:

"Ain't this cussed weather? Have yer even seen a fish this afternoon?"

He knew that I hadn't.

"Wel-el, I was sort of leadin' up to a point a while back, killin' two birds with one barrel, an'—"

"And," I interrupted, "that reminds me of something I have had in mind for two hours or more."

"What was that?"

"Let's go home."

"Go home! Why, it lacks two hours of night. Besides, we was goin' to camp out on the big island. It w'ud be pitch-dark afore we c'ud row down to the lower pond."

I agreed disconsolately.

"Fust off, I was goin' to suggest that we row over in back of the island. Maybe the wind ain't so bad in thar. Then we c'ud try some fishing."

For the time being, I had had all the fishing I wanted. The apple of it had turned to ashes in my mouth. But the idea of moving anywhere was inviting.

"Nobody," I muttered, "but a confounded fisherman would ever get caught outdoors in weather like this."

Dud bent to the oars. I envied him. Hunched on the back seat, I watched the shore line of the big island as we crawled along the bedraggled pond. A doe, wet but apparently happy, threw up her head and looked at us with amazement in her eyes. Perhaps she thought we were part of the dank fog that was puffing about on the lake. Thinking that the action would at least quicken blood circulation, I began to cast in toward the shore. The doe fled, tail up, with a thud of hoofs.

Dud paused at his rowing. "Thar's about three hundred acres, they say, in that island," he said. "Always is some deer on it. Once, I saw a bear."

My casting was fruitless. Dud rowed on, until we were passing around the north end of the big island. It seemed to me that the weather had grown steadily meaner. Now and then a drop of rain hissed in the pipe that I had dexterously lighted. Finally Dud pulled in the oars, and the sound of them falling against the boat rang across the whole lake.

"Mak," he began, "we've fished together quite a lot, an' I guess we can keep our own counsel. Look, I've got a box of them pop-bugs. The feller that sent 'em to me claims they're death on bass. Do ye s'pose they'd work on trout?"

"Sure, they'll work on trout—work better on salmon sometimes, but this isn't the sort of weather. We tried them out on salmon when the fish were feeding on the surface. Salmon knock the daylights out of those black ones. Trout like the browns. Sometimes they'll work when a dry fly won't.

"One night—gosh, Dud, but that was a wonderful night. There was a red sky that lasted for an hour or more. It just snuffed out, all at once, into darkness. Stars, big ones, melted through. It was soft and quiet and warm. It was nice in your shirt sleeves, and—"

"Never mind," interrupted Dud. "As the feller said when he had a bellyache, 'Don't talk to me about clam chowder.' Besides,

[80]

don't fergit that the next yarn is goin' to have plenty of rain in it."

And sighing rather prodigiously, Dud stuffed the little box of pop-bugs back into his pack and said reluctantly, "Wel-el, I warn't exactly goin' to mention it, as the feller said when he proposed to the old maid, but that feller also sent me three of these rigs."

When he removed the cover of the second box, I saw three objects about an inch long. One was white, one was black, and the third was brown.

"Holy Moses, Dud, those are mice!"

"Micers," corrected Dud. "Take your pick. They're fittin' bait fer a time like this."

"How have the mighty fallen," I muttered.

"No sech thing!"

I picked the little brown mouse as being, perhaps, the most lifelike.

"If it works," said Dud, "let me have a turn. We might's well be hung fer hoss thieves as jackasses."

I cast about thirty feet of line, dropping the bait close to the ledge that walls in the north end of the big island. After a few moments I began to strip in line. The creation moved toward us, looking very much like a live mouse on an aquatic migration. Dud watched intently.

When the trout struck, I was in the midst of a shiver that involved every muscle in my body. The strike, which was slow, startled me, and I jerked the lure away. The mouse hopped out of the water and came to rest about a yard ahead of the fish. It did not offer to strike again.

"Hold on, Mak!" chuckled Dud. "That's a mouse, an' not a bat. I'm afraid that leap fer freedom put that fish down fer keeps. An' that looked like a real trout. Why not fetch in that micer an' give it a rest? It don't seem logical to have mice as thick an' fast as a hatch of May flies."

I recovered the bait.

"Anyhow, that trout made me feel warmer," I said.

"Now try 'im ag'in."

I cast again, but there was no response.

"Crotch," muttered Dud in a frankly disappointed voice. "Try another hatch. Try this black 'un. Nobody ever saw a black mouse up in this neck of woods, but—"

"Let's try the white one," I suggested, "because it looks colder."

"Yer don't mean ye're feelin' cold ag'in!"

I continued casting the brown mouse. Nothing at all happened.

"Let's wait about ten minutes," said Dud. "Let's have us a smoke."

"Let's go ashore and build a fire."

"Crotch, we ain't got no time fer a fire now. Jist think how warm an' dry ye'll be when Gabriel blows his horn."

"All right, you take a turn at micing," I suggested.

"By godfreys, I will, but I'm goin' to try one of them nine-foot leaders. As fer them mice, guess I'll try the black 'un. Jist as soon, I guess. No, it's *too* black. An' that white 'un looks too white, seems so."

"Then why not try this brown one? It's too brown."

In a moment Dud stood up and cast the brown mouse out into

the narrow strip of water between the island and the mainland. "Jist like an owl had dropped it," he explained. "Mm, my pipe's gone out. Got a match?"

I offered my match case. Dud reached for it. Bang! The mouse shot up into the air. Dud reeled in several feet of line. Bang again.

"An' I hooked him that time, Mak."

A great salmon, nearly a yard long and thicker than any salmon I had ever seen, leaped straight up over the gray water. I uttered a meaningless ejaculation and gripped the gunwales tightly.

"How heavy is that leader?" I gasped.

"Aya," drawled Dud, "I had about the same idea myself. It tapers from b'gosh to I-guess."

As I grunted, "Good-by mouse," the salmon sailed out and down the channel toward the northwest.

"Ye mean, good-by micers," corrected Dud, and as he spoke his pipe fell from his lips into the water.

Hardly looking at it, I scooped it in with the landing net. The salmon had out more than twenty-five yards of line and was apparently plowing ahead to the bitter end.

"He's on his way," I said disappointedly.

"You fiddle while Rome burns, an' let's see what kind of a fireman I be. A fish ain't lost until he's throwed the hook; an' by crotch, that's a good-sized hook."

And at that remark the big fish slid upward, like a bright lance hurled aloft.

Dud chuckled. "Look at that old cuss shake hisself. Ain't that a fish? Ain't that a fish!"

"It's the best nonmigratory salmon I ever saw," I said.

"I w'udn't go that far," drawled Dud, "but if I sh'ud happen to git him in near the boat, draw a pitchur of him, Mak, becuz I'm beginnin' to be a little a-feared that we ain't never goin— Thar! What did I tell ye? By crotch a-mighty—"

"Is he—is he gone?"

"No, he ain't, becuz I read his mind an' had that slack ready."

"Read his mind!"

"Sartinly. A fish like that knows more 'n some folks that has wanted to run fer President. Thar! Jist look at that."

It was only one more wild and splendid leap, high and clear of the lake.

I exclaimed, "That fish will weigh fifteen pounds—at least!"

"He w'ud, if a feller c'ud ever git hold of him long enough."

To my surprise, Dud began to reel in line.

"Guess he's takin' a deep breath," he said by way of explanation. "Seems to be easin' up a little. Don't hang no part of yer over the edge of the boat, Mak. A fish like this is dangerous. I ain't had so much fun since the time Doc Brownin' fell off the boom-log. 'Stead of swimmin' ashore, he tried to git back on the log. Every time he got most of his heft on it, it w'ud roll, an' he'd pitch in on the other side. But he kept tryin' until he done it. Doc had a stubborn streak. An' what he called me an' the boom warn't professional. Right now that fish is a-diggin' fer bottom an' shakin' his head like a young pup that has jist met his first skunk. Thar he goes. Watch him, now. Don't let him git away!"

The salmon was surging straight for the ledge again. The line cut the water. Dud's face was again a-gallop with grins. "If he don't stop before he hits that ledge, maybe we can pull him out of the hole he's goin' to make."

It was a moment of crisis, and Dud put more strain upon his splendid rod than he had previously ventured. It bent like a gray birch with a small boy at its terminal.

"Crotch, Mak," muttered Dud, "now I am afraid that this leader *is* goin to hold, an' I'll bust my best rod instead. That fish intends to lick me. He's—"

Up came the salmon, in response to the lift of Dud's rod. And it fell back into the water like an inert thing.

"No, yer don't!" cried Dud in a tone of pure delight. "No, yer don't, mister. I never hooked a good salmon in my life that didn't try *that* trick before we was done. A little bit of slack line helps when a feller like you tries to fall smack on a leader."

Of course, the fish kept moving after the futile attempt to fall on the leader. In fact, once started, it came at us about as slowly as a cat out of a burning woodshed. And as it came abreast of the boat it pulled a brand-new stunt, so far as my fishing experience went. I suppose that it actually jumped about four times in rapid succession, but it appeared to be standing on its tail and to be propelling itself by churning that extremity much more rapidly than the eye could see.

It was, in fact, a most astonishing performance; and when it was over, Dud was standing with about eighty feet of line at his feet. For a moment we both stared at each other. It was a tense moment. Anyone who thinks that it is easy to hang to a fish like that for about thirty minutes, only to lose him in the end, is a ... I had every reason to expect a hearty chuckle, for I had often seen Dud laugh off events like that. But the laugh somehow didn't materialize. Instead, Dud's fine old face seemed to be set in lines which I interpreted as meaning that it had hurt to lose that salmon.

But my emotion of compassion was a gentle thing compared with my feeling when I beheld Dud clap his right hand to the vicinity of his heart.

"Take it easy," I urged in consternation.

"Huh?"

And he slapped both hands to the back of his hips. By that time I was sure that this was worse than the day when a good friend of mine actually sobbed on a like occasion. Dud's hand went back to his heart, and he looked off into the distance. There was no mistaking the utter gravity of his face.

"What," I managed to say, "in God's name, is the matter?"

"Matter? By crotch a-mighty, I've lost my pipe!"

"Pipe?"

At that Dud stared at me for a long moment, and then, like a sun over January hills, a laugh burst from his lips. "Oh, by Judas, I see what yer thought! Mak, I'm ashamed of yer."

"Well," I said recovering, "there's your pipe. I netted it when you dropped it into the lake during that salmon battle."

"Good! It seemed to me that I could remember puttin' that pipe in my shirt pocket."

A few moments passed, during which Dud soberly wiped out the bowl of his pipe with a white handkerchief and filled and lighted it. Then, assuming a tone of mock solemnity, he said, "Mak, the brown micer is gone ferever."

I nodded with equal solemnity.

"Aya, it's gone. Mak, I don't believe even some Presidents c'ud have landed that fish when it took to cakewalkin'. He caught me short, the old stager. The leader busted."

"We ought to try that white mouse in the morning," I said.

"Jist at daylight," agreed Dud.

VII

DUD GUIDES A LADY

SOME day," said Dan Nye, "git Dud Dean to tell you 'bout the time he guided a flapper down the East Branch. But don't tell him that I put you wise. Jist break it easy-like. It'll be worth a thousand."

So one night, when we were camping at Foley Pond, I broached the subject. I was comfortably arranged, and Dud's pipe was going nicely.

"Let's see, Dud," I began, "didn't you guide a lady, or something, down the East Branch one time?"

It was dark, but I could feel Dud's shrewd eyes turned on me. "What d'yer mean by *that*, er *sunthin*'?"

I had got off on the wrong foot. "Why, why, you did, didn't you?"

A half-moment passed, then I heard Dud's inimitable chuckle. "Maybe," he said, "I'll tell yer that adventure, if that's what ye're fishin' fer. But git this straight: she was a lady. By time! I've had trouble e-nough, settlin' that."

Then Dud went on with his story. Hereafter, Dud is speaking.

Let's see, time's draggin', an' you never did know enough to turn in. Wel-el, I'll begin it this way. That must of been the spring of 1913. Money warn't comin' in faster'n I c'ud use it; so I was pickin' up most any job that come my way. Erlong 'bout the fust of June, I got a crisp, short letter that said a friend had recommended me as a guide who knew the East Branch, some. An' w'ud I hire out to guide a party of one? It was signed, B. N. Turner.

Well, I read it over three-four times, an' showed it to Nancy. The letter was typewritten, by the way. Then I went down to Bingham station, an' got Pearl Woodard to fix me up a telegram sayin' the prop'sition looked all right to me. Next day, back comes an answer, tellin' me to be at Indian Pond, June fifth without fail.

"I hope Mr. Turner will be agreeable," says Nancy, when I was startin' out the day before the fifth, which w'ud be the fourth, like enough. By Jericho! If she'd known what I found out later, she w'ud have been real serious erbout *Mister* Turner bein' agreeable.

Wel-el, nothin' waits fer a man, but trouble, as old Doc

Brownin' useter say. I got everythin' fixed early the mornin' of the fifth. An' I had a nice, trappy little canoe I was real proud erbout. Of course I was feelin' purty good, becuz a party of one is easy guiding.

The train come in 'bout two o'clock. Fer a min-it, er so, nobudy got off, but I see a colored feller, a-pilin' off a lot of duffle; so I sorta eased up in that direction.

Then off gits a woman, 'bout twenty-five, I'd say. Crotch! Come to think of it, she might be almost a grandmother, now. She had on long yeller britches, an' a green huntin' shirt. She was a sight—a *sight*, I mean! Upon my word, that colored feller blushed, when he see me lookin' at the both of 'em. She gave him a bill. An' the conductor waved his hands. Thar we was, the flapper an' me, a-standin' all alone on Injun Pond platform. It warn't none of my business, as I see it, jist then, so I started to go over to the dam, where thar was some fellers workin' that I knew.

But she held up her hand. "Are you the guide, Dud Dean?" she asks me.

"Sometimes," I says.

"I am B. N. Turner."

Crotch, yer c'ud have used me fer log-chinkin'.

"But I was expectin' a man," I says, becuz it seemed like some explanation was necessary. Then I went on to say, "Instead of a—"

She cut me off short, like a kid that was speakin' out of turn at a Christmas exercise.

"I can't see that the fact I am a woman makes any difference. My money is jist as good. An' you have hired to guide me down

[91]

the East Branch. This is the East Branch, ain't it?" she says, wavin' her hand at the river.

"It is," I says, "but it w'ud take us more'n the rest of this day to make The Forks."

She kinda screwed up her face at that, like I had wandered from the subject, an' she c'udn't foller me. So I started in to clear up the situation, as Jim Perkins useter say, tellin' erbout some fight he'd jist got licked in.

"It 'ud mean campin' out two nights," I says.

"Oh," she says, sorta smilin'. I rec'lect that she was real purty, when she smiled, but that warn't often. Most of the time her face was like a starched shirt. "I brought my own tent," she says.

I had been lookin' at her baggage. It looked like a small circus outfit I once seen down to Bingham. So by way of bein' pleasant, I says to her, "Where's the wild animals?"

Wel-el, yer sh'ud have seen her scowl at me. "I find this banter silly," she snaps at me. "The question is: are you goin' to guide me down the East Branch, as you agreed, by wire, to do?"

"I am not," I says. An' I meant it. Why, gosh all-hemlock. It was the dumdest prop'sition fer them careful-goin' days. Ye've got to remember, Mak, that this was in 1913. Thar's a cool wind been blowin' sech foolishness out of the air, since then, an' I must say the air smells cleaner to me.

"Why not?" she shot back at me, 'ith her eyes lookin' right through me. "Is it ag'inst the law to guide a decent woman down the Kennebec?"

"Not if her husband—" I begins.

"Bosh!" she says. "Jist becuz you live in the woods, don't think that thar's stumps on Broadway. Rot! An' tommy-rot!"

"Madam," I says, "speakin' of Broadway, didjer ever hear of the Straight an' Narrow Way?"

Wel-el, thar ain't no sense in draggin' that out. Between you an' me, I was young an' reckless in them days. So I stored most of her junk in the drivers' shack, an' we got inter my canoe. Fust off, she was bound to string up a nice little rod.

You know the East Branch. Thar's some mean water in it. Fer one place, thar's the Hullin' Machine, an' a dozen more slipp'ry places. I had to carry 'round some. Then we'd ease down inter some of them nice pools. About two 'clock that mornin' they had shut down the gates at Injun Pond, an' the pulpwood drive was away ahead of us. Conditions was ideal fer fishin'. Thar was a chance fer squaretails, salmon, an' what not, as Doc Brownin' useter say when he was called out in the middle of the night.

When it come to fishin' that woman had everythin' I ever see hooked by the ear. More'n once she dum near hooked one of mine. But in them days good fly-men warn't so common, an' I was purty good at dodgin'. Fust off I tried to teach her sunthin' erbout the gentle art, but she w'udn't listen to me. A dozen times I had to yell at her, like the referee of a dog fight, to keep my canoe right side up. She was worse'n a monkey fer ballast.

An' mind yer, I never saw a better day fer fishin' on the East Branch. Thar was plenty of fish—plenty. Yer see a head of water slushes 'em out of Injun Pond.

Lots of 'em are Mooseheaders. It was strange that she c'udn't hook one. They'd roll up slow an' dignified. Then she'd fetch a squeal, an' a heave; yankin' the fly right out of their reach. I c'ud hear their teeth click.

Wel-el, along 'bout then she begun to drop some of her know-it-all an' own-it-all ways.

"Oh, darn," she says, "what shall I do?"

"Yer might stop yankin' your fly out of their reach," I says. But that jist froze her up, an' she turned her back on me. I never see sech a person. It took me all the afternoon to figger out jist what ailed her.

Bineby, while we was loafin' through a purty stretch of water, a nice little salmon, that 'ud go three pounds, maybe, lashed out at her fly. She done her best to yank it away from him, but warn't quick e-nough. He nailed that Jock Scott good an' tight. It s'prised her so, she dum near dropped her rod in the river. That's all that saved the rod at the start, I reckon.

Soon's she see her line a-swishin' through the water, she begin to pull back, but that didn't do no harm, becuz she never touched her line er reel. Gor-ry, but that salmon warn't long in headin' fer the next pool below us.

Anyone that knows me, knows that I ain't ever been able to take my fly fishin' like a drink of cold tea, an' I useter git real excited in them days.

"Git a hold on that line," I yells at her, an' at the same time I headed my canoe fer the rips.

That fish had some start on us, an' he was in the next pool, when we got thar. Then the fun begun, but all that flapper c'ud do was to squeal an' pull back on her rod. Thar was somewhere near ten turns of line 'round the bow, an' hanged if thar was any tellin' where the rest of it was, although that girl looked like a bobbin half unwound.

It was jist at that stage of the confusion in general that the fish begin to stand right up on his hind legs. "Oo-oo-ooo," she squeals.

"Tarnation!" I busts out. "Give me that rod! D'yer hear?"

It has always been my intention to be a gentleman, wherever, an' whenever, but I guess I fergot that I had a lady aboard. I purty nigh upset the canoe, myself, a-reachin' fer that rod. Fust thing I knew, I had it in my hands. I'd a looked less foolish if I had known e-nough to let her finish what she'd begun. With all them turns, bowlines, hangman's knots, sheep-shanks, an' what not, I had erbout as much chance of landin' that salmon as a deacon at a Democratic rally.

He fetched one er two jumps, an" was gone. It took me half an hour to untangle that line. While I was workin' away on the line, I heard a funny noise an' looked up quick. By gum if that flapper warn't bawlin'. I felt meaner'n a rabbit 'ith fleas, but I c'udn't think of nothin' to say.

Someone oughter write a book fer all young guides to study. Thar ain't nothin' from fust aid to funeral services that they don't need to be ready fer. Wel-el, bineby she slowed down some, an' seemed to change. I think she must have seen the pity in my eyes, becuz she got madder'n a set-on bumble bee, an' says with a voice that was shaky, but mean, "Ye're discharged!"

I was so dumfounded, I jist set an' stared at her. It was the fust time anybudy had ever tried to fire me.

"What?" I says.

"Don't you understand American?" she says, slow an' careful. "You are fired!"

I set out to laugh, but finally I says, gentle as I c'ud, "Now see here. I don't blame yer, Mrs. Turner. Naturally yer don't feel very good, but it's a long walk back to Injun Pond, an' I happen to be headed *down* river. Call it fired if yer want to, but I suggest that yer ride erlong 'ith me."

That woman had brains, of course. Fer a min-it, she sot an' looked at me, like I was the missin' link, an' turned what I had said over in her mind.

"Very well," says she, short, an' her voice under control ag'in.

I•finished reelin' up her line; threw her rod in the bottom of the canoe; an' dug the paddle deep. As I remember, I had some fool idea of reachin' The Forks b'fore sunset, which w'ud have busted a mallard's record, an' then some.

"Keep in the middle," I told her. "Don't throw your weight all on the one side. An' git your underpinnin' under yer."

Maybe that made her mad, I don't know. Anyway, jist as we hit the white water, an' I was diggin' to miss a nasty rock, she put her heft where it 'ud do the most good, from her point of view. All I c'ud remember, afterwards, was that I see the river comin' up inter my face, an' then it got dark, an' so still that I stopped hearin' anythin'.

The next I knew, I was layin' on some almighty hard-feelin' rocks. Fust off, I figgered that it was the bottom of the river, somewheres between where I'd gone down an' the Atlantic Ocean. But I put out my hands an' the rocks felt sorta dry. Then I begin to hear someone cryin'. "Can't be my funeral," thinks I, "becuz I can't smell no flowers."

Next I heard a voice, way off an' distant, sayin', "Are you dead, Mister Dean?"

I made out to answer, "No, marm, I don't think so, becuz I feel kinda chilly."

Yer see, I was gittin' some sense back. Fust thing I saw, when I opened my eyes, was a tree. It warn't much of a tree, but it had some sky behind it. So I set up. My head was sorer than a bobtailed pup. I s'pose likely I'd bumped it on the bottom of the river. Then I see her settin' thar—wet an' most of the starch gone out of her, by the looks.

"Where's the canoe?" I says.

"I hung onter that," she says. "It's d-d-down below here a little bit."

"Well," I says, "how'd I git here? Did I bounce here?"

"No-o-o."

I kinda felt all over myself; an' got up on my feet. Thar didn't seem to be nothin' gone, an' I was all in one piece. Well, two an' two is four, most gen'rally. She'd pulled me out, somehow. I took a squint at the sun, an' decided it was 'bout five. That gave us three hours, er so, of light. But we was in a pickle, jist the same. The grub I had brought along was in the bottom of the river.

We kept goin' till darkness had set in, an' then went ashore to fix up some sort of a camp. Nights git chilly 'long in June up in this country, 'specially if ye're damp. I had a knife, an' managed ter strip off some bark fer a lean-to roof. Then it came to me that my matches was all wet. Jumpin' hornpouts, talk erbout a gone feelin'.

I'm hanged, though, if that flapper, er flipper, didn't produce a dinky little watertight matchbox. I've never been 'ithout one since. In fact, the one I've carried fer years—no, never mind that. I got a nice fire goin'. But we had nothin' to eat. Which was tough. I made two birch-bark cups, an' a bigger dish ter heat water in. Yer can do it, easy enough, if yer don't let the fire git up above the water line. It tasted hot an' comfortin'.

Then we sot down fer a long night. After a while she begun to talk.

"I s'pose that you consider me all kinds of a fool," she says.

"No," I says, "I don't, but I wish yer w'ud tell me jist what your idea was in takin' this trip."

Wel-el, she jist wanted to git out an' see places like she had read erbout. That was all thar was to it. She was one of them females that had done too much thinkin' erbout the terrible injustices of a man-made world. One of them sort that think men w'ud still insist that their women wear veils, an' stay indoors, if they had their way. Never stoppin' to think that the days when women did wear veils an' stay indoors was the days when veils an' doors was purty essential. B. N. Turner, anyhow, had an ingrown idea that a woman was jist as good as any man, an' had set out to prove it. Which a min-it's reflection shows up to be a plumb foolish notion. I ain't never seen much real diff'rence 'tween a female an' a male. A mean woman's as mean as a mean man, an' a good woman is as good as a good man, if not better.

She told me that she didn't intend to give up her independence, jist becuz she was married to a man. That was the only real funny thing I see er heard durin' that trip. I've never noticed any of Nancy's independence oozin' away. We've shared an' shared alike. What we've got, we've got together. What we had to take on the jaw, as yer might say, we took together. If I wanted to go fishin', I went fishin', in spite of criticism. If Nancy wanted to go to a W. C. T. U. meetin' she went. An' I told B. N. Turner so. That seemed to interest her. She 'lowed that Nancy must be a woman with the modern point of view.

"Well," I says, "Nancy has always run her own affairs, 'ithout borrowin' my britches. An' that, young woman, is a text fer meditation."

Oh, I preached her a durn good sermon, if I do say so.

"If yer want to be a whale of a success, ye've got to work 'ith sech material as comes to hand," I says. "Wearin' yeller britches may be comfortable, an' sensible, but it don't fool nobudy—t'wouldn't if yer c'ud make your husband wear dresses. Most men ain't worth imitatin'. When women recognize that, they may git somewhere. Independence ain't a matter of yeller britches an' hard-boiled airs. Jist take dumpin' me in the Branch, which I don't blame yer fer doin'. To do that, yer had to dump yourself, an' your comforts. Strikes me," I says—Oh, well, I've fergotten jist what I did say after that. Never mind.

We set thar, an' shivered, an' dried out, fust in front, an' then in back. The fire got real warm, an' bineby I sorta dropped off to sleep. I dreamed that I saw Nancy comin' up the river in a canoe, an' she was lookin' fer me. After that I lay thar, kinda half awake an' half asleep.

Bineby B. N. Turner give me a shake.

"Wake up!" she whispers. "Thar's a puppy, er some dog, tryin' to come in through the back of this lean-to."

I set up straight. Ye've heard a wood pig, out in the night, kinda cryin' an' pleadin', like he'd lost his soul mate. "Scat out of here!" I says, throwin' a stick.

An' the last thread of that mask she wore fell off her face.

She had only sold herself on the idea that she was hard-boiled. She was jist a scared kid. Seems she'd been listenin' to that porcupine fer a long time. Thought it was a wolf, er sunthin'. Take almost any person, an' put 'em out in the deep woods at night, an' the veneer of civilization's assurances falls off. The night has a voice of its own, an' it has done me a heap of good to listen.

Jist to git her mind back to normal, I told her what I knew 'bout porcupines, which, if I do say so, is a lot more'n the average woodsman, becuz I'm one of the few that has taken the trouble to notice them. Most folks call 'em stupid critters, an' let it go at that. They do a lot of aggravatin' damage, like chewin' camp floors an' doors. Almost anythin' around a camp is splinters fer them. They damage an' kill some growin' trees. Our state paid a bounty on porcupines fer several years. I ain't sayin' the money was wasted. They do git purty numerous, by spells. But I do say that I c'ud have spent that money wiser...on house cats that have gone wild, an' half wild in the woods, fer instance. But never mind that. What I told B. N. Turner was erbout the amusin' tricks I'd seen porcupines do. Nobudy, nor no thing is as foolish as we're apt to assume.

Anyhow, I didn't sleep no more, an' I c'ud see that she appreciated it. So we got started down the river with the first light of mornin'. It's a nice ride down the East Branch. By crotch, it's beautiful! B. N. had washed in the river, afore we started, an' blamed if she didn't look kinda human-sweet, in the mornin' light. I drove the canoe fer all I c'ud. When we got down to The Forks, she asked me to find someone to take her right over to Moxie Station. Said that she c'udn't wait to git back home. Um... don't it beat all how I run on, when I git at a yarn?

I got Dan Nye to take her over to Moxie Station. When she left, out goes her hand.

"Good-by, Mr. Dean," she says, 'ith sunshine in her face. "You'll never forget this trip, will you? Neither shall I. Thank you."

I put my canoe in the Kennebec, an' went along down the river to Bingham. An' I'll bet ye're wonderin' how I squared all this 'ith Nancy. I'll tell yer 'bout that. Somehow, I c'udn't make up my mind to tell her, though I've always practiced bein' open an' above. Yer see, folks was awful set, in them days, on what is called conventionalities. It was jist erbout as bad to ignore them as to bust the Ten Commandments wide open. So I made up my mind to keep the whole business to myself. An' I'd already sworn Dan Nye to keep his mouth shut.

When I got home, Nancy says, "Well, how'd yer like Mr. Turner?"

"Wel-el," I says, "he was kinda s'prisin' in some ways."

Right then I see Nancy was eyin' my clothes, which was wrinkled. Anybudy c'ud see that I'd been in the water all over. An' Nancy knew it hadn't rained none.

"I sh'ud say that he was surprising," she says. "Can't you go fishin' without fallin' in?"

"I c'ud, but—"

"I know all erbout it, Dudley Dean," she snaps out. "You poor spineless thing."

Crotch, I thought I was in a box, if she knew *all* erbout it.

"Well, Ma," I begins, but she w'udn't let me finish.

"How much did *he* pay you?"

"Who?" I says, kinda blank like.

"Who w'ud I mean, but this man, B. N. Turner?"

"Oh," I says, "twenty dollars."

Wel-el, that kinda salved Nancy.

"That," she admits, "is good pay for two days, if only you had backbone e-nough to leave liquor alone."

That smarted me some, becuz I ain't never messed 'round with booze, but if she wanted to think that I'd fallen into the river in that way, I decided it was all right.

Maybe ye're wonderin', if Nancy ever did find out the difference. Wel-el...you know Nancy.

VIII

BASS ARE BASS

"HOW about some bass fishing?" I asked Dud, one suggestive morning in June.

Dud Dean simply shook his head.

"Why not?"

"Jist ain't interested. Never see a bass, as I rec'lect."

"But it is said, that pound for pound—"

"Aya, I've heard that one, an' it don't sound reasonable to

me. Thar ain't no pound of nothin' that can put up a bigger an' better show 'n a white-water salmon."

"Get your rod," I challenged, "and I'll show you that the black bass need not dip his colors to anything that swims."

But Dud simply leaned back against one of the shade trees along our main street, and began to fill his antique pipe.

"Look here," he said, squinting at the sky. "I can see that ye're itchin' to go fishin', Mak, an' I know where thar's some prime salmon jist waitin' to grab a Jock Scott. I mean *salmon*, mind yer!"

I countered with, "A fellow just told me about a pond where we can catch black bass—bass that will outstage any of your salmon." You see I wanted to inveigle Dud. A day's bass fishing with the old veteran promised so much.

Dud stared at me. For a moment his sense of humor was paralyzed. I had blasphemed against his prince of fresh-water fishes.

"By crotch, Mak, yer can't mean that! What's chewin' in your head?" Then, recovering from his shock, he added with a grin, "Mak, I'm 'shamed of yer."

"But," I persisted, "you wouldn't deny a fact, would you? I am offering to prove that pound for pound—"

"Crotch, Mak, a fish ain't a fact. It's a fish. A whole lot of foolishness c'ud be avoided in this world, if folks w'ud keep their facts an' fish separated."

Well, it looked as though I were trying to drive my logs against a head wind, as Dud would have put it. "Hang it all, Dud," I said, "I want to take you bass fishing. Try it once!"

"How many miles is it to this bass pond of yours?"

"It's over in the back part of Solon—say, ten miles."

"As near as that? Fust thing we know, somebudy'll be plantin' them warm-water fish up here. An' I've been given to understand that they're sunthin' desperate on trout. Which puts me in mind of what Hen Barnaby told the jedge when he fined Hen for contempt of court. Says Hen, 'Mister, thar ought to be a law ag'inst sich a blarsted outrage.'

" 'That'll cost yer five dollars more,' says the jedge, 'an' every time yer open your head ag'in, it'll cost yer five more'n that.'

" 'Kin I ask jist one question?' says Hen.

" 'It is irregular,' says the jedge, 'but I'll permit it.'

" 'What I want to know is,' says Hen, 'are you God Almighty, er jist a plain two-legged critter like me, only a darn-sight meaner?' What I was thinkin' of was that thar ought to be a law ag'inst puttin' them bass—"

"But what do you say?" I broke in. "Will you give the bass a tryout?"

"Wel-el, ter tell the truth, I d'know but that I'd try most anythin' right now, becuz Nancy's gittin' worked up fer another house-cleanin'. It's in the air. She's sniffin' out the corners, an' squintin' erbout fer imaginary cobwebs. D'know but I'd go cusk fishin' to escape that, although cusk fishin' is so low-down that it's ag'in the law in Hell Huddle, an' sh'ud be everywheres."

And so it came about. When Dud showed up, he was carrying his best rod. That was significant. But he persisted in maintaining his skepticism of bass.

"Yer know, Mak, I feel ornery," he said, "I feel as low-down as I did the day I skipped school, years ago, an' found out in the afternoon that it was a holiday, anyway. Here we be, you an' me, goin' bass fishin'. The mighty has fallen flat, as Doc Brownin' useter say."

I passed that off with a grin. I could afford it. I had accomplished my objective that day. Once on the road an expression of deep contentment settled over Dud's fine face. And as we rolled along the road, I fell to thinking about the many trips I had enjoyed in the company of this mellow, home-town philosopher. I have spent many days a-field in such good company.

A chuckle interrupted my reveries. "I was jist thinkin'," Dud explained, "erbout the fust automobile Nancy an' me bought. Prob'ly yer ain't noticed it, but Nancy has got opinions of her own. One of 'em is that a woman can do anythin' a man ever done, an' do it better. So when automobiles came erlong in this country, it galled her awful to hear folks talk as if no woman c'ud ever learn to drive one. An' she got it inter her head that we'd got to have one. At fust, when she brought up the subject, I argued that I c'ud never learn to drive one of them things. But that jist made Nancy look scornful.

"Wel-el, bad news blows wherever it listeth. An' one day a feller come to our house, all dressed up like it was Sunday. He was sellin' automobiles, of course. The one he had was all trimmed up 'ith brass an' do-dads. The bulb on the horn was most as big as a football. Nancy was taken 'ith the looks of the whole rig. She took lessons on it, till finally that slicker told her that she c'ud drive it as good as any man that ever come down the pike. That clinched the deal. I fergit what the whole thing cost, but we bought it.

"A few days after that, Nancy an' me started out. We got erlong slick as a beaver, at first, but everythin' we met had a

devil of a time. Fer instance, we met old Ben Hall comin' erl
leadin' a black an' white cow. I was scared, becuz it looked
Ben an' the cow warn't never goin' to turn out.

" 'Blow that horn,' I says. 'That's what a horn is fer.'

"Nancy musta been a little scared herself, becuz she did
what I told her to do. I never saw a cow as quick as that or
She jerked Ben right off his feet, an' the gol-darn idgit hung
the rope. The last I see of them, Ben was wrapped 'round a
apple tree, but the cow was jist goin' over a fence in the nex
field.

"Nancy never said a word, an' we kept right on, like nothin'
had happened. Bineby, I see that we was comin' to a bad turn
in the road ahead. An' we was goin' so fast the tears was runnin'
out of my eyes. Crotch, we must have been goin' twenty miles
an hour!

" 'Here comes a turn,' I sings out. 'Look out fer that bad
turn in the road! Slow down. D'yer hear?'

"If she slowed down a mite, I c'udn't see it. But I guess that
she w'ud have made that corner, if she had changed the wheel
after we got 'round it. But she didn't.

"Thar was a nice little white house on that turn. An' it had a
white picket fence eround the front yard. We went through
that fence like it was built of match sticks. Thinks I, 'A fence
like that is no protection at all.' An' the next second we hit the
house sunthin' wicked. But it never budged a bit.

"It was a Sunday afternoon, an' the old couple that lived thar
came runnin' out, 'ith their arms up in the air, like they was
willin' ter surrender 'ithout an argument. But when the old
feller see that it was us that had hit his house, instead of sunthin'

supernatural, he begin to swear. He was a pitchur, 'ith his long hair a-wavin' in the breeze. An' his flow of language beat anythin' I ever heard, except Doc Browning's. Thar was a while when I thought that the old codger had an edge on Doc, but he got to repeatin' hisself, 'long at the last. I guess he had the talent, but lacked Doc's eddication.

"Nancy's hat was down over her eyes, but she give it a poke, and when she see where we was, she acted like somebudy had played a dirty trick on her. 'Dudley,' she says, 'git down an' crank this machine.'

"So I climbed down, an' cranked. An' that automobile started like it had never stopped. I got in ag'in an' Nancy got all set ter back out. She tramped 'round on them pedals, like an organist gittin' ready ter play the Lost Chord. An' we backed out of that yard as neat as a crab c'ud. Then we got stalled ag'in, afore Nancy had got straightened away. So I got down, an' cranked some more.

"By that time, a crowd had gathered from nowhere. Thar was a lot of loud talkin'—most of it from the old feller, who hadn't run down none. I s'pose it all made Nancy nervous. Anyhow, she stepped on a pedal, intendin' ter back up a little more. An' by crotch if we didn't shoot back inter the yard ag'in. An' if we was goin' twenty miles an hour, when we hit that house the fust trip, we was doin' thirty when we struck it the second time.

"The old lady of the house had been down on her knees, sort of moanin' over a bed of red geraniums we had run over on our first trip in. She never had no time to straighten up, but jist crawled out of our way by the skin of her teeth.

" 'Thar, by gad!' yells the old man at her. 'Yer git inter the house, er they'll kill yer!'

"But I can't say that even the house seemed like a real safe place ter me, by that time. I warn't jist calm after we'd fetched up, an' I says ter Nancy, 'If ye're goin' to do that ag'in, I'm goin' to git out an' walk home.' Soon's I said it, I was sorry, becuz I see that Nancy was 'bout ready to bawl.

"Jist then, a young feller stepped up an' says, 'Havin' some trouble, er jist tryin' her out?'

"By crotch, that was jist erbout the last straw, as Dan Nye said, tellin' how bad his hay fever had been, an' I was jist a-goin' to git out ter show that young squirt sunthin', when he added that he was an automobile mechanic, which was what we needed, as sure as a ship ever needed a sailor. Wel-el, he offered to back us out an' git us squared off fer home. Which he did. Then he offered to drive us home, but Nancy 'lowed that she was perfectly capable from thar on, thank yer. After we'd gone a few rods, I begin to git back a little confidence. An' by crotch if we didn't sail erlong nice, until we got to our house. Seemed like stoppin' was one of Nancy's troubles. So we rode inside the barn, 'ithout openin' the doors. An' the blarsted thing never stopped, until we fetched up ag'in a post."

We were going down Gilman Hill, when Dud finished his story. One gets a partial view of Iron Bound Pond from that elevation.

Dud, who apparently had not noticed the road, while he had been recalling his first automobile trip, sat up straight. "Why didn't yer say we was comin' over to this pond?" he demanded. "I've been told that thar's some good salmon in this water."

"Bass, too," I added.

We left our car at the foot of the hill, and then walked down to a black, weather-beaten house, where, I had been informed, we might hire a boat. The negotiation was simple. And at the landing we picked the most attractive craft. Dud took the stern seat, asking, with an oar poised paddle-wise, "Where?"

I explained that I had been instructed to fish the lower end of the lake; that the bass were supposed to favor that section.

"They w'ud," grunted Dud.

But in spite of his show of indifference, I noticed that Dud toyed with his nice rod, as he put it together.

"A split bamboo," said my old friend, "is a great contraption. The other day I was readin' a list of great inventions. The feller that made it up, claimed that each invention he listed had turned some tide of hist'ry, but the gol-durn chump never mentioned the split bamboo."

I passed my fly book to Dud. "Here are some bass flies," I said, "which are also great inventions."

Dud looked at the bass flies dubiously. "They look like I expected," he said. "An' they ain't fit to put on the end of a light leader, let alone usin' on a good rod. Guess, if you don't mind, that I'll stick to my own. I'll jist fool 'round 'ith a Jock Scott. Maybe thar's some *real* fish somewheres erbout this pond."

I selected a bass fly with a silk body, bound with silver, and wearing regulation wings and hackles. Dud watched me, out of the corner of his eye, but continued his own beautiful casting without further comment.

The next two hours seemed to confirm my opinion that our cold-water bass would not take a fly, although I had been assured that they would. We moved about, but hung to the lower end of the lake. Finally Dud remarked, with evident disappointment, that the salmon must be few and far between in Iron Bound Pond.

"Maybe I had better try one of them frog-ketchin' rigs of your'n, Mak. I jist see a fish feedin' over by that bunch of grass, but most likely it's nothin' but a pickerel."

Again I offered my fly book.

"These ain't flies," Dud muttered, "but here goes, as Clum McGlouster said, time he fell off the barn roof. Is this here thing s'posed to float, er sink?"

I turned to inspect the fly he had picked out. It was one that a friend had tied, and he had used the tip of a red squirrel's tail, with a bit of hackle from a white Leghorn rooster. All in all, I felt compelled to admit it the most unlikely fly in the book.

Without waiting for a reply to his question, Dud cast. "It's floatin' purty good," he commented.

"Let her float," I said.

Dud twitched the fly lightly. Something swirled up from the deep water. Spray broke, as though a miniature depth bomb had gone off, and a nice little bass smashed Dud's fly on the rise. For a moment the fish stood out against the afternoon light, vibrating from gills to tail. Then it hit the water, tossing the hook from its mouth.

An odd look of surprise appeared on Dud's lean face. "The low-down tud," he muttered in an undertone.

Then he addressed me. "Turned that trick purty slick, didn't he? Guess I'll have another try at him, like Doc Brownin' said, time a three-year-old colt kicked him flat."

Dud dropped his next cast upon a small stool of grass. At a hint from his rod, the fly dropped into the water. Nothing happened, although the thing had been perfectly done, and Dud said with a ludicrous trace of anxiety in his voice. "Yer don't s'pose I gummed up the works, do yer?"

And at that moment I connected with a two-pound bass—not a big bass, but a bass. As Dud said, later, "A hooked salmon kinda scoots up inter the air, like it knew jist how it oughter be done, but a bass jist rears up an' let's her go, like it didn't care a dang how it's done."

When Dud had netted my fish, he examined it with interest. "By crotch," he muttered, but volunteered no more. I looked off to the east, grinned, and winked at nothing in particular. And then we continued our casting. Presently I hooked another bass, but fumbled it. And soon Dud took a bass that would weigh a pound and a half. As I netted it, I looked to Dud, supposing of course that he would direct me to turn it loose.

"Dang it, Mak, I know what ye're thinkin', it ain't big but I aim to keep that bass. Some of the fellers might want to look at him. Yer know, it's been a month of Sundays since a fish slipped me as neat as that fust big 'un did."

The fish that Dud referred to could not have weighed over two pounds, but I refrained from saying so. Dud was warming up to bass fishing! But the day was far spent.

It is superfluous to mention that spell which haunts the woods and inland lakes at twilight. Night and day are one for a moment. Day lingers. Night procrastinates. Lights become duns. Colors of sunset become diluted tints. Sounds assume a new resonance, with the harsh notes whittled down. The day balances its books, and turns over the accounts to the night and the stars. Twilight is the prelude before the deep rest from growing toils. It is the return of the eternal lull.

"Geehosaphat!" exclaimed Dud. "Did you see that?"

It was the swirl of a mighty fish in the dark water.

"Ain't that a sight! Right under our noses! It was a salmon, er maybe a trout. Acted ter me like one of them old bottom sinners that cruises up once in a blue moon ter see if the sky is still on top of the world."

As he talked, Dud pulled out his own immense fly book and searched through its pages.

"Ten to one," I said, "it was a black bass."

Dud did not look up, but said, "Guess yer didn't notice that fish, Mak. It was a fish that 'ud weigh five pounds er more... Now here's a female Black Gnat—black wings, white edges. That's a nice fly, Mak. Bright colors fer salmon, sure, but don't fergit to try a Gnat, now an' then."

"For trout, maybe, for salmon, sure, but for—"

Dud interrupted me. "Aya, for salmon, sure!"

"It's a total loss," I said.

"Fer how much?"

"Any amount, if you want to gamble."

"Sish. Make it ten thousand, Mak."

Of course I couldn't stand a figure like that, even in fun, but before I could alter it a startling commotion occurred in the vicinity of Dud's fly. In fact a he-fish had smashed Dud's Gnat, as though it were a tiny ship, riding at anchor with all her lights hung out. Fish like that do not come often, in these days, for the simple reason that it takes several years to raise one. When

[113]

Dud set the little hook, the fish plunged away like a heavily loaded ferry boat. But please don't let that figure convey the impression of ungainliness!

"Whoa, thar!" said Dud. "You ain't goin' inter them bushes if I can help it. Dog-gone it, Mak, why don't I have more faith, er less confidence. I've gone an' put on a leader that's too light fer a fish like this."

The bass came out of the water, tossing itself into the air like a punted football. For a brief moment it stood out in the twilight.

"If that ain't a fat salmon, I'll eat him," drawled Dud. "Them black salmon is always bottom feeders. He's loaded heavy, an' he fights deep. Seems like he's got a whole bagfull of new tricks. Right now, I can feel him standin' still, an' shakin' his head, like a dog 'ith canker in both his ears. Acts like he was mad as a forked bull."

The fighting fish was beginning to rush circles about the boat. Dud was busy gathering in line that he must soon allow the fish to take again. But Dud was having a big time. Grin after grin chased across his face.

I waited for the remark I had heard so many times, under similar circumstances. At last it came:

"Crotch, Mak, this fish thinks it can git away from me! Hope that hook don't wear a hole in his mouth, an' fall out. Got to keep a tight line, if he ties me up in a hundred knots. Seems like I never see a salmon pull so. Yer can see it ain't no bass, becuz no bass 'ud last this long, even if I can't put all the strain on him that I w'ud if I had a fittin' leader. Nothin' in fins can match these salmon. Cousins, they are, to the kind that useter run up from the sea. Great fish they was, Mak. Grand fish, they be!"

I kept my peace. In that half light, I could see the grin etched all over Dud's face. Now and then he blew great gulps of air through his lips, tilting his gray mustache askew.

"Mak, I ain't had so much fun, seems like, since the fat lady, over to Embden Fair, tipped back in her chair an' fell off the platform. Look at that cuss toss his head, when he comes up to swear at me."

I uttered an enthusiastic tribute. "It's a fine bass!"

Dud was as near to anger as I ever saw him.

"Holy Moses, Mak! That ain't no bass! Stop sayin' it, er I'll be mad at yer, fust thing yer know."

I watched the fish break and leap a half dozen times, thereafter, but each smashing plunge upward occurred in the shadows, and I could not be sure it was a bass. Still the tactics were reminiscent of bass. And I held, in silence, that it *was* a bass.

The battle began to lag. "I'm afraid that it's sunset an' evenin' star fer this fish," said Dud. "I hate to lick 'em, an' I hate to git licked. That's fishin'!"

There were a few more dogged plunges, and an abortive leap, and the old warrior rolled on his side at the surface.

Dud swung him into the boat, where I could easily reach him with the landing net.

"See," I said triumphantly, "it *is* a bass!"

Dud stepped to the middle of the boat, and we both looked down at the beaten fish. "Must be a salmon," he insisted.

"Look at it!" I exclaimed.

Dud got down on his knees, to see his fish the plainer, in the dim light. "Shucks," he grunted, "I thought it licked too easy fer a salmon."

I carelessly slid the net toward the fish.

"He's all done," said Dud, "but save him. I want to show him to the boys. Some of 'em never saw a bass."

Then a coiled spring seemed to let go in that bass. An astonishing explosion of energy occurred. Dud and I threw back our heads, but Dud's face got a liberal splashing of pond water. Getting to his feet hastily, he exclaimed, "By crotch! What swallowed that fish?"

But of course the spurt of life was short, and that game old bronzy had to come in at last. Again I slid the net under him— that time cautiously—and lifted him into the boat.

Dud sat down, wiping his face.

"Have you got that bass? Can't get away to save hisself, can he? Licked, ain't he?"

"Absolutely," I answered.

"Well, then, by crotch, is he dead?"

"No, but I'm going to hit him over the head with this paddle."

"No, sir! Don't yer do it! Gol-durn him! Let him go! The old son-of-a-gun."

Feebly moving his tail, his gills working gaspingly, the old bass sank out of our sight. The inky waters welcomed him home again.

"Thar!" said Dud. "That's over. But jist the same, I'd have liked to show him to Nancy. I don't s'pose she ever see a bass."

"Can a bass fight?" I asked.

"Well," began Dud, as he took down his rod, "that reminds me of Robby and Mike Fitzpatrick. They bet on a dog fight. The dog that Robby picked had some advantages.

" 'By the lovely, lovely,' says Robby, 'my dog licked your'n.'

" 'By the roarin' Jorus,' says Mike, 'not from where I was standin', he never!' "

"But," concluded Dud, "it's up to me to say that a bass is a bass. An' what d'yer say if we try 'em ag'in, some day?"

IX

A MOONLIGHT CANNONADE

DUD DEAN and I sat on the porch in front of the old office of the Depot Camp at Austin Pond Station. It was a half hour to twilight. We had come out from Bald Mountain Pond. There was a pleasant day of fishing behind us.

"Look at them rabbits," said Dud, pointing with his pipe.

I looked. There were at least six brown-coated varying hares, chasing each other in the lush grass about the old horse hovel.

"Them," declared Dud, "are the queerest critters the Almighty ever furnished 'ith grass an' fodder. Take the name, rabbit. It has come to stand fer sunthin' that is simple and timid. But as a matter of fact, they ain't timid at all. Rabbits an' women is somewhat alike. Women are commonly 'sposed to be timid, but looks is deceivin' and so is a rabbit. In spite of the fact that they're three meals a day fer wildcats, foxes, weasels, an' owls, thar ain't anythin' I know better equipped to take care of itself 'n a rabbit.

"Take their feet. I suppose that the average, full-grown snow-shoe rabbit don't weigh much over two pounds, although some bucks might weigh a little more. But if yer stretch out a hind leg, ye'll find that it's twelve inches long, an' jist erbout the most powerful rig fer runnin' that was ever contrived. Measure their hind tracks, an' it will surprise yer. They're five inches long, when the foot is spread out. Snowshoes!

"I never had a chance to git a check on a rabbit's speed, but it's my opinion that nothin' on four legs can catch 'em, when they've decided to go somewhere else. Sh'udn't be surprised, if one of them jumpin' jackasses c'ud hit up to sixty miles an hour, fer a ways. Sartinly a feller must lead a cross shot, if he expects to hit one that's turnin' up the flats of his feet. That's what makes rabbit shootin' good sport. They've got more shifts an' speeds than anythin' that runs to git away. Each shot is a problem that has to be solved on spur of the second.

"They've got speed. An' yit, their gait is so deceptive that a greenhorn w'ud think that he had time to light his pipe. They've got smooth, easy action. An' if a man wants rabbit fer supper, he had better shoot an' do it quick. He can light his pipe on the way home. The sum an' substance of it is that most charges of shot land where the rabbit was.

"A rabbit is a dumb critter fer anythin' that knows so much. Thar ain't no predictin' what's next. One min-it, your bunny will be kickin' out at top speed. The next, he'll be settin' on his tail. He'll go by a given p'int like he was headed fer Canada, an' the very next moment, he'll come back an' squat down right where he was when he left. Or maybe he'll race off fer a mile er two before he comes back. An' if he does come back, it's becuz thar's a good dog a-drivin' him.

"More'n once, I've seen a rabbit come a-rippin' erlong 'ith the hound dog hot behind. All of a sudden, it w'ud turn an abrupt angle off the trail. Then the hound w'ud plow right by, an' like as not that snowshoe w'ud jist set an' watch the hound go past. An' by the time the hound had the matter puzzled out, the rabbit w'ud be off fer other places. Then too, if thar's a hard place fer a dog to git through, a rabbit is sure to lead the way as easily as sunthin' that's greased.

"Nature takes all the colorin' out of their fur, when cold weather sets in. But sometimes they git a raw deal. The weather gits cold, but the snow hangs off. At sech times, game wardens sh'ud hang up lookin' glasses, becuz them rabbits don't realize that they show up like a white feather in a black hat.

"But when the snow an' that white hair come the same time, a man can't hardly ever see a snowshoe, unless it moves. Still, they don't seem to have e-nough patience to keep still fer any length of time. They'll always wiggle an ear, er scratch 'ith a hind leg.

"The p'int I had in mind was that they're a puzzle nobudy can figger out. Seems like that they've got long sensitive hind legs an' ears in place of real good brains. So it can happen that nine times out of eleven they're where they ain't, an' ain't where they are, when yer look fer 'em. They look as sweet an' gentle as a lily, but they fight among themselves like a pack of devils. They act as if they was scared of a shadder, but, actually, they ain't a-feared of anythin' under the sun. That's all that keeps them from overrunnin' the earth.

"They are careless one min-it, an' careful the next, which puts me in mind of the time I went down to Boston. I had been in a place fer a snack of sunthin' to eat. When I come out on the street, I looked up to see the biggest woman I ever laid eyes on a-bearin' down on me. I turned to the right, an' she turned to the left. An' so we come tergether. Then I dodged to the left, an' she rolled right. Crotch, we kept up that wewawin' until I was dizzy.

"I guessed it pervoked her. 'Well!' she says. 'Why don't yer go on your business? Are you afraid?'

" 'No, marm,' I says, 'jist tryin' to be careful.'

"Rabbits is careful by spells.

"I'll never fergit the fust time I tried huntin' rabbits. Thar was a feller by the name of Anthony S. Dunnivan that got me inter the scrape, and, on an' off, I've been mixed up 'ith it ever since. He was a manufacturer of alarm clocks, er hair mattresses, I fergit which. Anyhow, he had made a lot of money doin' it. So, yer see, that was some years ago. I guided him that sum-mer—up in the Enchanted country and we got plenty of nice trout.

"That summer, rabbits was uncommon thick. They're that way some years, an' some, they hain't. Everywhere we went, we'd see rabbits. If we sot down on a log, out w'ud jump a rabbit. An' jist at twilight, ye'd see lots of 'em settin' in the tote roads. Dunnivan c'udn't git over how plentiful they was. I told him that anywhere I'd been that spring, thar had been as many.

" 'Yer don't say!' he says. 'By George, I'm comin' up to see yer, this winter. I've got the best rabbit dog that ever yowled and I want to try him.'

"Of course, I didn't know he meant it, an' so I never give the promise another thought. It didn't seem reasonable that anybudy in his right mind w'ud come away up here to go rabbit huntin'. Thar warn't a soul eround here, in them days, that ever dreamed of goin' rabbit huntin' fer business. But, by crotch, erlong in November, I got a typewritten letter, sayin' that he was comin', although I warn't to expect him until he got here.

"Wel-el, sell me short, as a feller I guided last summer kept saying, if this Dunnivan didn't make good his word. One afternoon, I was out in the shed, buckin' up wood, an' sort of prayin' that some interruption w'ud happen. I looked up, at the sound of footsteps, an' thar it was.

" 'How's your rabbits?' asks a voice.

" 'Huh?' says I.

"An' then I sort of took in the pitchur, as Jim Brown said the time a moose put him up a tree. Thar was Mr. Dunnivan, an' another man who was jist erbout the fattest man I ever see. Besides them fellers, thar was a big black an' tan hound, that was the saddest lookin' dog I ever seen.

"At fust I didn't pay much attention to the dog, becuz, in them days, a rabbit hound was a good dog that had gone wrong —a hound that had been born on the square, but was doomed to die 'ith an inferiority complex. I got that last word from a book Nancy read out loud. It was erbout rights fer women, an' what's left, fer men.

"But when yer did look at that hound of Dunnivan's, yer felt like cryin' yourself, er like kickin' him under the tail. Upon my word, that dog had the most woebegone face I ever see. He looked like sunthin' that had been through hell an' back.

"Wel-el, Dunnivan an' his friend sot down, one on the choppin' block, an' t'other on the steps that led up to the back kitchen door. Jist then, Nancy's big cat came out from some-wheres. To tell the truth, I never liked that cat, an' w'udn't have cared if sunthin' accidental had happened to him. He put up his back, an' walked right up to that Dunnivan hound. Then Nancy's tomcat squared off, quicker'n a common cat, an' fetched the dog a mean rake across his face. Ye sh'ud have been thar, an' a-heard that dog yowl.

"Nancy come out the kitchen door, 'ith a broom in her hand. Dunnivan an' the other feller got to their feet in a hurry, but the hound jist sot thar, lookin' neutral an' innocent. Fer all Nancy c'ud make out, it was me who had done the bellowin'.

"I interduced them to Nancy, an' she took her cat, which had mounted the woodpile, an' went back inter the kitchen. So we sot down ag'in. The fat feller'd held in, an' now he let her go. The tears run out of his eyes, an' the front of him rolled up an' down, like he had stuffed a mess of floppin' fish under his vest.

"'Well,' says Dunnivan, 'how about the rabbit hunting? Hope there are plenty of them left, becuz I don't want Ralph, here, to call me a liar when we git back.'

"Tarnation, I felt foolish. I looked at my watch, an' it was almost five o'clock, an' gittin' dark.

[124]

" 'Too late, today,' I says.

" 'Oh, no, it ain't,' says Dunnivan. 'Thar's a full moon to-night. We've got to get back in a day or so. I've hunted cotton-tails by moonlight, many a time. It's tricky shooting, but thar's no reason why we sh'udn't have some rare sport up here. Of course, if your eyes ain't sharp, an' yer can't hit where yer shoot, thar's no sense in it. They go by like shadows.'

"That last crack sort of nettled me, to tell the truth, becuz I had always aimed to shoot 'ith the next feller. An' even if I didn't, it was always hard to admit it. Matter of fact, I reckon I never grew up on that score. Still; I didn't feel drawn to this rabbit huntin' prop'sition, peeticularly in the moonlight.

" 'Wel-el,' I says, 'it's ag'inst the law to hunt with any sort of a light up here in Maine, but maybe the game wardens 'ud stretch a p'int on moonlight. I d'know.'

"That made them fellers laugh, but when we went in fer supper, I called up the local warden. Now, it beats the dickens, but most anybudy knows all erbout the game laws, er thinks they do, but a warden ain't hardly ever prepared to be so blame positive.

"Our warden said that he didn't know whether it was legal to hunt rabbits by moonlight er not, but that he was danged sartin it was a crazy idea—bad e-nough by daylight. Old Ben Osgood was listenin' in on the line, an' he butted in with, 'Thar's a full moon tonight, Dud.'

"I had the satisfaction of askin' him who had rung his number.

" 'Wel-el,' he says, 'I was jist wonderin' if yer realized that somebudy might see yer.'

"Of course, what Ben had to say didn't affect me none, but

jist the same I did hate to go, an' I made considerable talk erbout how cold it was. But them fellers laughed that off. An' by gum, I had to go.

"It was a wonderful night. The air was clear as brook water. The moon was as big as a hogshead, an' as yeller as a buttercup. It seemed like I had never seen sech a moon in all my days. I took my little sixteen doubled, an' *plenty* of ammunition. Dunnivan owned a twelve-guage pump gun. His friend had a handsome little twenty. It was a beauty, but I wondered if a man c'ud hit a white rabbit in the moonlight 'ith a gun like that.

"Dunnivan's fat friend got behind, goin' up the pasture. While we was waitin' fer him, Dunnivan told me that his friend was the best wing shot in their club. I thought he'd need to be.

"Let's see, I hain't mentioned the dog. They had him on a string, but it didn't appear that the precaution was necessary. He was jist trailin' erlong, an' actin' like he wished he was back in New Jersey. But when we got to the edge of the alders an' stuff, Dunnivan turned him loose. I recollect that he called the hound, Singer, after a sewin' machine, I guess.

"The melancholy critter didn't act much good. Jist sot down an' looked at us, as if he was tryin' to figger out which one of the three was the most complete idgit. An' when Dunnivan told him to git busy, he jist looked up at the moon; looked at it kinda long an' thoughtful. Arter maybe ten min-its, I reckon he concluded that it wan't nothin' good to eat, becuz he begun to sniff and snuff the snow he was settin' in.

"'That means he's goin' after them,' Dunnivan explained. 'And what we need is a nice open place, where the rabbits are sure to cross. Know such a place?'

"That was easy, er it w'ud have been in the plain daylight, becuz all we had to do was go up the pasture hill a piece, where thar was more er less open pasture. But thar was a patch of thick cedars between. Did yer ever try walkin' through cedars in the moonlight? Wel-el, they ain't so bad as thorn plums. To make it as easy as I c'ud, I followed up a little brook bed. Mr. Skinner, that was the fat feller's name, broke through the ice. The way he acted, the water must a been wet. I told 'em that settled it. We'd have to go back home, becuz Skinner w'ud freeze his feet. But, no, sir, they w'udn't listen to any sort of reason. I 'spose a man needs to be half crazy to make a fust-class rabbit hunter, anyway.

"Anyhow, we hadn't but jist got through them cedars, when the hound busted out. It was a sudden experience. Yer felt like yellin' at the dog, 'Hush up!' Fer a few seconds I thought all hell had broke loose on us.

" 'Do yer hear that?' says Dunnivan. 'Singer's got one goin', by golly!'

"So we hurried fer the open land. The snow thar was criss-crossed with rabbit trails. An' each of us picked out a likely place. Meanwhile, that hound was more than whoopin' it up. An' I had jist got my feet placed, when his noise was comin' straight up the hill at me.

"Thinks I, 'Now be careful not to shoot Dunnivan's dog,' but that warn't necessary becuz the rabbit seemed to have plenty of headstart. I hain't sayin' that it's so, but it sartinly seems as though a rabbit c'ud run faster at night, jist as that hound bayed louder'n any hound I ever heard in the daylight.

"I kept an anxious lookout. Fust thing I see was sunthin' that seemed to be flyin' low, jist above the snow. It looked all the world like a small ghost. Looked like a haunt, a-floppin' erlong the snow. I felt like a man that was gunnin' in a graveyard. Crotch.

"I pulled up an' took good aim. After I pulled the trigger, thar was nothin' to be seen of that rabbit. The dog came plowin' erlong past me, an' I jedged that rabbit had gone on his way rejoicin' that I was a bum shot. I waited to hear them fellers open up, but I guess they didn't see the rabbit, which warn't to be wondered at. After the dog had gone over the ridge, he sounded away off and weird. Made me wonder if he was chasin' anything real.

"Then Skinner called down to me, 'Did you git that one?'

"'Nope, I didn't,' I says. An' I heard him chuckling.

"'If you fellers w'ud keep quiet, over thar,' says Dunnivan, 'we might git a crack at a stray one.'

"I never said anythin' but I figgered it w'ud have to stray in slower'n that fust one, er I warn't apt to hit it. Then maybe ten min-its passed. It was mighty white an' still, except when Skinner stepped eround to keep his feet from freezin'.

"Purty soon, I heard that hound. An' he was comin' up the hill at me. How in time he got back eround thar, I don't know, unless he had spells of still-trailing. I stood thar, listening, an' wishin' that fool dog w'ud take his rabbits some other way. But I p'inted my shotgun on the spot where this rabbit had come through on the fust trip, becuz I had always heard that rabbits returned by the same route. But d'ye think this one did?

"The fust thing I knew was a kinda thump-thumpin' on the snow, but I c'udn't locate nothin'. While I was squintin' this way an' that, the hound opened up, right near me. Crotch, that rabbit had been settin' within ten feet of me! All I saw was a blur of white. But I let her go, same's a man w'ud at a quick wing shot. That snowshoe never stopped. He turned on another notch of speed. When I got the gun on him, thar was a birch tree, a foot through, smack in the way. An' that was the last I c'ud see of my rabbit. Singer, the hound, went boomin' by me, like I was so much scenery. Then I heard Mr. Skinner open up. He got in two shots. Then it was still, aside from the sound of the dog goin' over the ridge ag'in.

"It was Dunnivan's turn to ask who had the luck. 'Did you git him?' he says.

" 'No,' says Skinner, 'but if he comes up here ag'in, I'll catch him in my hands.'

" 'I mean the rabbit,' says Dunnivan.

" 'So do I!' says Skinner.

"Maybe that hound lost track of his rabbit. Anyhow, bineby we heard him comin' straight back, down the hill. This time, he was headed fer Dunnivan's end of the lot, an' I felt easy. That twelve gauge made an awful racket in the night. The dog stopped howlin', and I wondered if maybe Dunnivan had made a mistake.

" 'I hit him!' shouts Dunnivan.

"An' I concluded that he must mean the rabbit. Thinks I, 'Now, maybe they'll be willin' to go home,' but they didn't mention that. Maybe ten min-its passed, an' Singer begun to sing ag'in. He was trackin' back an' forth in the black cedars below us. While he was yowlin' back an' eround ag'in, I leaned back ag'inst a little maple. Fer the fust time, I noticed how purty it was our in the woods beneath that white moonlight. I saw a black shadder floatin' over the snow, and, lookin' up, saw a big white owl. I set out to shoot at it. Them ar'tic laddies raise the dickens in these woods. Then it come to me that he was huntin'. An' so was I. I let him go, untroubled. If it had been daylight, I might have killed him. Maybe I warn't confident that I c'ud have hit a large barn. My shootin' had kinda undermined my sartinty.

"Wel-el, I was thinkin' how different, an' strange, things looked at night, when I'll be hanged if my eyes didn't make out another snowshoe. Instead of comin' up er down, like the rest, he was amblin' across the lot, towards me. He didn't seem to be in a hurry, er to be goin' anywhere in peeticular—jist out fer the romp of it.

" 'Mister,' I says, 'ye're a dead rabbit, er my name ain't Dud Dean, an' I never shot a gun.'

"I follered erlong, an' led him jist a trifle. Of course thar was an up an' down to his gait, but it w'ud have been a beautiful shot, if he hadn't sot down all at once. It beat me. He didn't put on any brakes, but jist stopped short, when I was pullin' the trigger. Crotch, that moonlight shootin' was sunthin'!

" 'Git him?' shouts Skinner.

" 'Yep,' I says, but what I meant was that I intended to git that rabbit 'ith the second barrel. An' I was takin' pains, too. It was goin' to be an awful crime—shootin' that white cuss while he was settin' still, but that was my aim an' design.

"But when I had pulled the behind trigger, I see that thar was some mistake. Thar warn't no rabbit. When I had squinted some, I made out that I had shot at a rock with a cap of snow on it.

" 'Well,' says I to myself, 'that's dum strange. Fust it's a rabbit, an' then it's a stone.'

"So I went over to view the situation. When I got almost to the rock, the rabbit, which had been a-settin' within ten feet of my mark, lit out of thar, like I had done sunthin' to offend him. I pulled on him, but I had neglected to reload the gun. Crotch! I was out of patience!

" 'Did you git another one?' yells Skinner.

" 'Naw,' I says.

" 'He missed that one,' Skinner shouts to Dunnivan.

"It struck me that they had a rotten bad habit of talkin' back and forth, like they was out fishin' er sunthin'.

"Wel-el, I walked back to my post. 'That one,' thinks I, 'must have been one of them strays. I'll wait till that bellowin' dog drives up a reg'lar one. It won't git through here, unless it's over my dead body.'

"Then, somehow, it came inter my head that if a man was to git down on his knees, he c'ud see better. It was peeculiar, but jist at that min-it, here come another rabbit. He was dustin' up the trail, the same trail over which the others had come. I was ca'm as an owl. Jist pinched on the right trigger. Tarnation, it beat all. Near's I c'ud make out, I blowed up a lot of snow in that rabbit's face. I had undershot.

"The foolish thing jumped up in the air three feet, an' lit a-runnin'. 'No, yer don't!' I says, talkin' out loud. An' I had the gun dead on him. I jist c'udn't miss. But when I looked, he warn't thar, nowhere! I w'udn't believe my eyes.

"Whang goes Skinner's gun, an' he shouted over to Dunnivan, 'One I got, one you've got, one Dean's got. That makes three.'

"It made me feel right-down foolish. Dean hadn't connected, yit. Thinks I, 'It's three, if your'n is twins.'

"Honest, Mak, I felt awful. It don't seem possible an old idgit c'ud git so upset over missin' rabbits. But a man's pride is his foolishness. An' that hound jist didn't know e-nough to git discouraged. He went castin' erbout, an' purty soon, sure enough, he was tonguing another snowshoe. He drove that one down the hill, an' Dunnivan took both barrels to stop him, but he did.

"I fell to thinkin' erbout other places, an' I moved over on the other side of the open space. That is, I walked across maybe a couple acres. On my way over, I looked at the place where the rabbit had seemed to be, when I had tried the second barrel. Thar was alders here an' thar in that lot—not growin' thick, but old an' tall. In the moonlight, it was hard to tell which was an alder an' which was its shadder. If it had been a shadder, I w'ud have hit that rabbit.

"Anyhow, thar was rabbit paths all over that lot, an' I picked me another likely stand. An' I waited, grim as the white owl is on nights like that. Once Singer went a-boomin' up the old path I had quit. Skinner was likely unprepared, when it passed him; and it must have give the hound the slip, over on the other side of the ridge. He came back, sniffin' and snuffin' through our clearin'. The rabbits was gittin' purty spread out, an' he grumbled erbout it.

"It come to me that what I needed was a smoke. So, after a while, I begun to fill my pipe. It was fittin' that sh'ud be the time fer Singer to chase a rabbit up my way. But nothin' happened fer a space. Then, it did. The hound warn't a hundred feet behind his rabbit, an' he was a-roarin' like a county commissioner. As fer the snowshoe, anybody w'ud have thought this peeticular rabbit had been shot out of a cannon.

"I had the moonlight clear erlong the barrel of my gun, but I let fly 'ithout aimin' much, same's I w'ud have done in the daylight. An' i-jing, that feller doubled up in a heap. Of course I c'udn't see it in the snow—but I saw it plain e-nough, when it got up an' lit out ag'in, like nothin' had happened except the noise the gunpowder made. And, as a matter of fact, I had run over to pick up my game. So I was some nearer fer the second attempt. If intentions ever killed anythin' I sartinly didn't need no number sixes. I was as mad as Obijah Goodrich.

" 'Git him?' says Skinner, curious as ever.

" 'Yes, by crotch! I got him!' I says.

" 'An' I want yer to understand that I hadn't exaggerated none. Yer might have picked up e-nough rabbit fur to fill a sleepin' bag. An' the odds an' ends was distributed all over the landscape. That cuss was left lookin' like Humpty Dumpty. All the king's doctors an' all the king's specialists c'udn't have put it tergether ag'in.

"I was pervoked. That warn't the reason, of course, that the moon slunk behind a cloud, but it was sartinly suggestive. Anyhow, it got too dark fer rabbit hunting.

"It was time to go home, anyway. But do you think that black an' tan w'ud quit? Not much! The last we heard of him, he was humpin' another rabbit right up the path where I had been standin'. I 'spose he wanted to see if I c'ud do it ag'in.

"When we got home, Nancy said that the game warden had called up three times, since we had been gone, an' that he'd left word fer me to call him when I got back. So I done it.

"'That you, Dud?' he says. 'I looked up my book, an' near as I can make out, it's ag'in the law to hunt anythin' after sundown, so it's illegal to hunt rabbits, too.'

"'It oughter be,' I says, an' hung up the receiver."

X

RED FLANNEL

U P in a mountain range, west of the Kennebec, there is
a little lake known only to local fame. The natives call it Spruce
Pond. And round about it the spire spruce stand watch, while
the white pines croon the old, old song of the wilderness. I have
not studied that brand of psychology which maintains that
certain personalities have some dynamic spark about them usually
described as "it," but I can avow that out of the two or three
thousand lakes in Maine, some are just lakes, while others have
"it" at the heart of them. This mysterious distinction might be

traced to several sources, the chief of which is the lure of big trout. I have listened to many a theory set forth to explain why the trout in some waters never grow to weigh over half a pound, while in others, no fairer to the eye, they attain weights which make the fisherman's heart flutter.

Spruce Pond has been stocked now and again. There are two distinct types of trout in it. The stocked trout is just a speckled fellow, but the old strain is different. It is native to Spruce. His sides are pink. He is dotted with tiny pin-prick spots of fire-red. I have seen prettier trout, but none I had rather thrash on a four-ounce rod.

So much for that, and for the motive of Spruce Pond expeditions. As for the route—there are two. One chooses to walk up either side of the mountain. He walks. There are camps; a cabin and a woodshed. Sleeping and eating quarters belong to Zack. And he doesn't care whether anyone comes or not. He is not in the business of waiting on "sports" or anyone for that matter.

Trout fishing shuts down tightly in Maine on the first day of October—the day ruffed-grouse hunting opens. The last fifteen days of the season are fly-fishing weather. I met Dud at Ben Adams' barber shop one of those mornings.

"Dud," I said, "I want one more fling at the trout, before I varnish the old rod, and put it away for the winter."

"Tell yer, Mak, I'm kinda ag'in this fall fishin'. Been hopin' some smart member of legislature w'ud fix it up so us fellers w'udn't git tempted 'long toward spawnin' time."

"But I'm going after a specimen," I explained. "I want just one of those Spruce Pond trout. They're distinct—almost a sub-species."

Dud grinned at me. "Wel-el, Mak, if that's what ye've got in mind, I d'know but I'd go yer on it. I ain't been up to Spruce fer three-four years. It's a purty little pond. An' I'd like to see old Zack ag'in. Zack is a mighty fine kind of a cuss at heart, but he ain't never admitted it. Aya, I'll be danged if I w'udn't like to talk 'ith Zack erbout this'n that."

And so we loaded our packs with food and blankets, and started for Spruce Pond on the fifteenth day of September. It was *more* than three miles from the point on the old Canada Road where we left the car to Zack's camp. The sun was warm, and we perspired frankly. When we came, a little wearily, to our goal, there sat Zack. He sat on an ancient chopping block, pipe burning lazily, with a rapt look of meditation on his sharp face.

If I ever have the time and the courage, evenly mixed, I will ask Zack about his earrings. Earrings! They are about three-quarters of an inch in diameter, and of gold wire. I am certain that they are not for ornament. Zack doesn't run to trappings and vaingloryings. I suspect that they are some sort of charm to keep off disease.

"How-they-bitin'?" asked Dud, as we came to a halt before Zack.

Zack surveyed us dispassionately, and asked, "What in tarnation be you fellers doin' up here?"

Dud and I displayed our rods.

"Eh? Well, they ain't bitin'. Thank God. Yer might's well go hum."

"Not bitin' at all?" questioned Dud.

"No, they hain't."

"Oh, come on," chided Dud. "Dave Beane said that he got a dandy mess up here, day 'fore yesterday."

"Did, did he? Wel-el, he likely got 'em somewheres else."

Zack spat savagely.

Dud and I slid off our packs.

It is no secret that Zack has a pronounced weakness for pork sausage.

"I brought up three pounds of sausage," I remarked.

Zack surveyed me impersonally. "Judas!" he said from between his teeth.

And that left me in the dark. I wondered if he was thinking of the small price paid Judas, or whether I reminded him of that trader in silver.

"Sausages ain't much good, from my standpoint," exclaimed Dud, " 'ithout a fry of trout to go with 'em."

Zack swung on Dud. "Judas! I'd like to see yer git them!"

"How about your boat?" I ventured.

"It's down't the pond, but it leaks like a young'un," grunted Zack.

Dud and I started down to the pond.

"Where's them sassage?" Zack called after us.

"In my pack," I said. "What fly did you say the trout were taking?"

"They hain't takin' nothin'. I'll fry them sassage up fer yer— 'bout sundown, maybe."

"Sure. Wish you would, Zack."

Dud and I paddled out on the little lake. It was as blue as a roadside aster, but as noncommittal as a deaf and dumb politician. I claim to know something about big trout ponds. Not much, mind you, but this much: maybe the *big fellows* will come to your fly and maybe they will not. Big trout ponds are all alike—uncertain as army mules.

Dud and I began casting flies. We cast to over there, and from there back again. It wasn't monotonous, because every once in a while a good trout appeared on the surface. Now and then one leaped playfully over our leaders, like a grammar-school girl jumping rope before her first love. The trout were not at all serious—just playfully energetic.

That sort of fishing is all right for a while. But a man's leader doesn't need to be soaked longer than two hours. We worked hard at the game. At the end of a season, a fellow's fly book sports an array of flies. I tried everything in my book, but a Red Ibis. I have frequently noticed that anglers form somewhat un-reasonable prejudices against certain flies. Of all the flies I know, the Red Ibis stands at the foot of the class. It will work wonders in a beaver bog of small trout. That is exactly what it stands for in my line-up—a beaver bog fly. So of course I did not try the Red Ibis. It remained in the book, dry and brilliantly exclusive.

But after many flies, Dud tied on a Red Ibis. At the first cast, he hooked an eight-inch trout. He removed the Ibis, shaking his head.

I went on casting and changing flies. There was a nice ripple although the sun was bright. If I can't hook fish at all, let it be on a warm comfortable day. Nothing continued to happen. Dud exploded. "I can stand this sort of thing in June, an' never turn a hair, but I'll be hanged if it ain't tiresome this afternoon. Mak, the thing that provokes me is that I'm willin' to bet all the t'bacca I've got with me that old Zack knows exactly the fly that'll make 'em set up an' pay attention. By crotch, it makes me kinda wish I'd kicked his pants years ago."

"Why?"

"Why? Becuz the old weasel is holdin' out on us."

I was considering that, when a voice called down to us. "Them sassage is erbout done."

Dud chuckled, slapped his knee and said:

"Mak, I've got it! Let's you an' me pretend like we was plannin' to eat them sassage ourselves. That'll fetch Zack round, until he'll be ready to eat out of our hands er to blow our heads off 'ith his old shotgun."

We went up to the shack. It was four o'clock anyway. In the cabin, a platter of sausage reposed in lonely grandeur. Dud and I extracted bread and extras from the packs. Sitting down, I said to Zack, "Pull up a chair, and have a *lunch*."

"No, I hain't hungry. Et sunthin' myself."

"Oh, have a sassage," urged Dud.

Zack produced a tin plate, and I forked one sausage, brown and sizzling hot, on the plate. The plate lingered for more, and I piled on two slices of bread. Zack glared at me, but fell at the food. The sausage disappeared first.

"Now, Zack," began Dud, "what're they takin'?"

I held my fork over the sausages; ready to spear one. Zack eyed my fork with a hopeful glint in his black eyes. "I tell yer," he said, "that I hain't tried 'em, lately. Last time, it was a Coachman."

I unloaded the sausage on my own plate. We had tried Coachmans. "Um," I said, "these are good. You fry 'em to a bull's-eye, Zack."

"Judas!" muttered Zack, stuffing a half slice of bread in his mouth.

"A Coachman," said Dud, "is a good fly, sometimes. Sometimes it ain't. How do yer like them sassage, Zack?"

"I've seen better, an' I've seen more."

Dud looked out of the window, by which he sat.

"The trout," he announced, "is jumpin' now'n then. If we was reasonably sure of gittin' some, thar's that other bundle of nice sassage, that 'ud do fer mornin', but we ain't sure, so I s'pose we'd better go out tonight."

"Might's well," I agreed; spearing another sausage; and watching Zack out of the corner of my eye.

"Ye might try a Parm Belle," Zack suggested. But that didn't ring true, because Zack knew that Dud and I would not be apt to forget the Parm Belle. However, I speared a sausage. Dud held out his own plate.

"Be them sassage made of native pork?" Zack inquired.

"No," replied Dud. "Why?"

"Didn't know but they might be. Seems like thar's a lot of hogs kept in Bingham."

"When did yer say yer tried them trout last? An' what was they takin'?"

"Night 'fore last. I'll take another—"

"Piece of bread? Sure, Zack. Mak, give Zack another piece of that bread. Give him some of those doughnuts. Er w'ud yer rather have some jellyroll?"

"Judas," muttered Zack. "Jellyroll, Judas!"

"Now what else was they takin,' night afore last, Zack?"

Zack stood up, glaring at Dud. "Red flannel, ye condemned fool! What else w'ud they be takin' these cold nights?"

Zack's voice, which had been loud and angry in the foregoing, now took on an ironic tone. "Yer set up to be a guide, yer do! Got a ceetificate from the state, most likely, I bet. Bet it says that ye're a registered guide. Registered jackass!" And he finished with, "Take them sassage an' feed 'em to the fish, condemn yer."

As Zack stood there, gripping his tin plate, the plate shook like a poplar leaf in a gale. There is a legend that once upon a time Zack lost his temper. That was years ago, before he came to live at Spruce Pond.

I hastened to pile the remaining sausages upon Zack's plate. For a moment, they were in danger of skidding off to the floor. They actually danced around on the plate. But the sight of them seemed to calm Zack. "I've got a good notion," he informed me, "not to eat a consarned one of 'em."

"Pshaw!" drawled Dud. "Did yer want some sausage, Zack? Why didn't yer say so, er help yourself?"

Zack sat down, sputtering something about old-fashioned manners, and the days when men were men.

"So they'll take red flannel, will they?" asked Dud.

"Not off'n a durn fool," said Zack.

"Where w'ud a feller git a yard of red flannel?"

"Judas Priest!" ejaculated Zack, gripping his plate with both hands, and half rising. "How sh'ud I know. A yard, Judas Priest!"

"Where did yer git yours?" persisted Dud, winking at me.

"Pulled it off my shirt, of course!"

"Ours ain't red," sighed Dud.

Zack turned on me. "Supposed to be a man of kind an' gentle ways, hain't yer? Crotch! Take this ladies' guide out of here this min-it, b'fore I murder him."

"No joking," I said, "what fly would you try, if you were going fishing tonight?"

"I hain't jokin'! I got 'em on red flannel, like I said. Cut some little strips and wound it on a gut hook."

"We ain't got any flannel," moaned Dud, who would have scorned to employ Zack's flannel.

That was doubtless too much. "If yer wasn't a fool, altogether, from Genesis Chapter One to Revelations Chapter Twenty-two, ye'd know that a body hain't botherin' with red flannel, if he's got any Red Ibises."

"Red Ibis!" I exclaimed. "Why, that's the last bet on a three-legged horse."

"Yes," scornfully replied Zack, "an' the fly-fishin' is two-legged, spavined, an' ready to bury."

"Zack, do ye *mean* Red Ibis?" demanded Dud.

"Ju-das," moaned Zack. "Hain't you a keen cuss? They'll be runnin' yer fer gov'nor, er sunthin', next."

And Dud and I knew that we had the truth from Zack.

The late sun was pelting gold leaf at the water when we went down to the lake again. A black drake and three ducks cut their way, unconcernedly, through the precious stuff. We paddled Zack's old tub of a boat out into the pond.

"Sunset—all yeller like that—reminds me of fools' gold," said Dud.

"I've noticed it many a time, when I've been fishing," I confessed.

We tipped our naked leaders with a bit of crimson feather. Spurning the gold, we cast into the black water and shadows. For several minutes we were unable to coax a response. A trout broke, over to my right. I was so anxious that the line and leader splashed out loud when I cast at the boil. The fish broke again, nearer the boat. I stripped line, and tried once more. There was no response.

"Oh, heck!"

I began to cast aimlessly toward a small stake, driven into the bottom. Up came an old whale of a trout. Down he went, and missed the Ibis. I put the fly back in the same place. Plop. He struck lazily. "All right, Mister," I said, and cast several feet to one side. "If you don't want—"

Wham!

"Crotch," exclaimed Dud.

That trout came to the net. It was a little fellow, comparatively —weighing about a pound. "Stocked trout," said Dud, and liberated the fish.

Apparently the trout liked that water in the vicinity of the stake. I flung out the crimson lady. She nestled beside the stake. I skittered her coquettishly through the zigzag shadow of the mark.

Smash! One never forgets that sensation. Once it happened over at Island Pond, in Ten Thousand Acres; again, it happened at Pierce Pond. It happens a few times in the life of every persistent fisherman. It hounds a big thrill down a fellow's veins. It is the big moment when the *big* trout strikes.

The old fellow showed himself again and again on the surface. What a fish! Give me a trout and choose what you will. I was sweating with the sun gone, and a September chill stealing over the water. It was a long, stubborn tussle, but at last the old soldier rolled up, beaten. I worked him to the net Dud held out with carefull skill. His great, broad side was almost as red as the Ibis he had tried to smash.

The next moment the water boiled. And he was gone—gone, taking the scarlet lady with him. I eyed the ripple, and my teeth were on edge. Dud did not utter a sound, thus proving his right to a guide's license. But Zack spoke, from the boat landing. "Hah, huh."

Thus the scenes shift in life. I looked at Zack sorrowfully. "Zack," I said, "he would have weighed nine pounds."

"Huh!"

Zack was getting ready to do some fishing himself. In his hand was a beautiful rod that some "sporter" with an enlarged heart had given to him, after a day of memorable fishing in Spruce. I watched Zack, listlessly, until I saw him produce a large Red Ibis... not a piece of red flannel.

"Crotch, Zack," called Dud, "I really w'ud be ashamed to wear an undershirt like that. Puts me in mind of...never mind, I'm 'shamed of yer, Zack."

Zack paid no heed to Dud, but began casting a long line out into the pond. The next moment the water boiled about his red fly. And Zack began to conduct his own one-ring circus. Envy blurred my eyes, but I knew in my heart that Zack was a master at his trade—which it was, quite literally. Surely he was twenty minutes bringing that trout in to the boat float.

"I've got five dollars here I'd like to give to any worthy cause, if Zack sh'ud fumble that trout," said Dud chuckling.

But Zack didn't fumble. He bent his six feet of leanness, and reached out a long finger, hooked it into the trout's gill, and held up the old he-fish for our consideration. And it seemed to me that against that weird twilight background of black fir and spruce, Zack was like an ancient priest of the night. I caught my breath, for a second, and expected him to break forth in chant.

He did. He uttered a sound three letters long: "Huh!"

XI

THE LATEST DOG

THE last kindness of the October sun touched the wide valley of the upper Kennebec. It was a stone's throw back to summer, and a toss to the white months of winter. I took my hat and set it on my head, and started upstreet in search of Dud Dean. It was high time to get out in the hills, where the ruffed grouse were drumming in the lazy autumn air.

Mrs. Dean surveyed me with critical eyes. It was apparent that she suspected truancy. "No, Mr. Macdougall," she replied, "Dudley isn't at home. He went down to Whitney's store to get some putty. I told him that this nice spell of weather was just the time to get the storm windows on for the winter. He usually puts it off until it's so cold that I pity him. I presume that your storm windows are all on, aren't they?"

I was considerably embarrassed, and was glad to escape Nancy's half amused and half censorious eyes. Muttering something about wanting to see Dud for a few moments, I hastily retreated.

I met Dud on his way home. He carried a small can, presumably putty, in his left hand, but he had forgotten it. In fact he did not notice me until I spoke, and my greeting interrupted a profound consideration of the frost-painted hills. My hound dog goes out in the yard, throws up his head, and sniffs the weather. Dud seemed to be doing much the same sort of thing.

"Nice day, Dud," I said.

"Aya," he replied, bringing his gray eyes to rest on me. "Aya," he reiterated, looking off beyond me.

I grinned, rather sheepishly. It seemed probable that Nancy's storm windows would wait for less auspicious weather.

"Aya," repeated Dud, "did yer see the latest setter?"

"Why, no. Your wife didn't mention a setter. She seemed to be interested in—"

"Hm. Sh'udn't wonder. Never mind that. Come up and see the latest. Ain't really looked at her, myself. Jist came on the mornin' express."

"Well," I began, hesitatingly, "we really should get started. You go up and get your gun and dog and meet me down here at the corner."

The lines about Dud's eyes danced merrily. "What'll I do

with this putty? Wish I'd fergot the danged stuff. Tell yer what, you come up an' help me smooth Nancy's fur down. Or be yer nervous?"

"I am not. Why should I be nervous?"

"Um, wel-el, I never heard of putty sp'ilin'. So, by crotch, I'll go yer! Git that old omnibus of yourn, an' me an' the dog'll be down here waitin' fer yer. But we ought to pick out sunthin' kinda special. Know where thar's some nice flocks?"

"I know where there are a half dozen, and some woodcock to boot."

"My gosh, Mak, that sounds good enough. What more c'ud a mortal ask?"

So we got going.

"Tell yer what," said Dud, as he climbed in, and we started out with his latest setter, "next to trout fishin', I'd as soon gun fer pa'tridge. They're smart. The Almighty made 'em early in the mornin'. It's danged wicked, an' all, to say it, but as long as I can lug a gun, an' October comes round once a year, I ain't hankerin' to graduate. Once, when I'd been uncommon mean, Nancy allowed that I warn't fit fer heaven.

"'All right,' I says, 'let 'em leave me right here, till I be.'"

"It surely is a great afternoon."

"Crotch, Mak, yer ain't strong on language, be yer? Why, the weather today is almost as good as it feels."

"What about this latest dog?" I asked.

"She's one of the same old breed, Mak. Ain't had her out. What erbout them pa'tridges yer had in mind?"

"Well," I confessed, "they're tamish, I'm afraid. The sort that like to *run* out of trouble."

Dud chuckled. "I like 'em wild, Mak. An' say, that puts me in mind of the time Hen Withey an' his wife went to Skowhegan Fair. Sadie always kinda hung onter Hen, though why nobudy else c'ud ever guess. Wel-el, Hen an' Sadie wandered erlong the white way, which was erbout as white as Hen's shirt. They followed the crowd, which is dum dangerous, an' fetched up in front of a tent that had the usual platform in front of it. The en-tire company was on it. Thar was a feller in a wrinkled dress-suit-case suit, four or five this er thats an' a girl with as little on as the law allowed.

" 'Come, Henry,' says Sadie, tuggin' on his arm, 'this ain't no fit show fer us.'

"She was agitated an' talked purty loud, an' her talk attracted the passers-by. Hen was as stubborn as a skunk. He allowed as how he was goin' to stay right thar an' listen, seein' it didn't cost nothin'. Their chewin' back an' forth drew more of a crowd than the barker had, but Sadie kept tuggin' on Hen's arm an' sputterin'. Finally, Hen got real exasperated.

" 'What have yer got ag'inst this show?' says he.

" 'Henry Withey,' says Sadie, mighty tight lipped, 'them is wild women in thar.'

" 'Well, crotch,' sings out Hen, 'I like 'em wild.'

"Erbout that time, that gal sort of two-stepped up erlong side of Hen an' Sadie, an' fetched a kick that sent Hen's derby a-spinin' off his head. If she had kicked him in the face, Hen w'udn't have been more surprised. 'By crotch a-mighty,' says Hen, dustin' off his hat, 'yer didn't need to take me so gosh-durned literal, young woman.'

"Maybe that's the way I feel erbout the pa'tridge. I like 'em wild, but not too wild. When they take to flyin' out of a lot b'fore a man c'ud throw a baseball in the front—

"Well, here we be, danged if we ain't, as my friend Humphries likes to say. Yer know, I kinda figgered we both had the same birds in mind. I see 'em, when I was fishin' up the brook last August. Let's see, that fust flock was hangin' out down in them alders, warn't they?"

As we got out of the car, Dud looked at the latest setter in a puzzled manner. Then turning to me, he asked, "Now what in Tophet is this dog's name? Prince Step-and-Take-It? No, that was the big raw-boned feller I had two falls ago. Let's see—last fall it was Pride of sunthin' er other. Gol-durn it, I've gone and fergotten this dog's name. Here you, Bill Barnum, the third, er whatever, git goin' an' show us if ye're any good in this country. Yer better be, becuz if yer ain't, we'll have to stay home an' put on storm winders."

"By the way," I said, while slipping shells in my gun, "just how did you arrange that matter?"

"Oh, I hired the young feller next door. He's goin' to git married, sooner er later, if he keeps foolin' around, so it's good practice fer him. Yer might say that it serves him right. G'long, Bill."

At that, the big setter looked long and thoughtfully at Dud.

"Well, how c'ud yer expect me to remember that?" he demanded, as though the bitch had asked him a pointed question. "Mak, it's jist come to me that this setter's name is Lady Gracious of Kennetunk. So now that's been taken care of, suppose we git goin', Lady G."

The setter raced ahead to the alders.

[151]

"I'm afraid she's too fast," said Dud. The words were but spoken, when the big setter came to an abrupt halt and a beautiful point.

"Crotch," whispered Dud, "Lady Gracious, sure e-nough!"

I offered, none too obviously, to fall behind Dud. He motioned for me to come abreast.

"Don't sneak out of it that way," he said, with a deep-throated chuckle. "I always dread terribly to be responsible fer the fust bird of the season. Every fall, I feel jist the same way I did when I toted my fust muzzle-loader. My heart goes plunkity-plunk, an' I'm scared to death fer fear I'll miss the fust shot."

We were walking up to the setter. In front of her was an island clump of alders, such as one often sees in old pastures.

"Pshaw," muttered Dud, "I'm afraid that's one of them woodcock of yourn. If it is, you shoot him."

I walked closer, for I knew that Dud felt woodcock were a little beneath his gun. A small brown bird shot up out of the alders, and away into the heavier growth beyond. It left a faint swirl of whistling sounds in the October air. The setter stood her ground. Somehow I had not been able to get my gun on the bird.

"Deuce take them little whistlin' idgits," drawled Dud. "I 'spose yer c'udn't see him, c'ud yer, Mak?"

"Certainly I could see him—more or less."

Dud laughed softly. "Mak, maybe ye're like me—got a one-track mind. Likely, yer was thinkin' pa'tridge. Then up gits one of them little long-nosed pokers. It ain't fair. We might's well raffle off our guns an' join the army of the unemployed. Lady G., this is ruffed goose country—that's what Dan Nye useter call

'em. I'd jist as soon yer'd stick to pa'tridge, an' let them doodle birds go on south. An' furthermore, yer don't need to look at Mak, like he was the fust feller yer ever saw do a thing like that, becuz we know ye're lyin'.

"Crotch," continued Dud, "I'm beginnin' to be afraid that Bart has sent me a dang lap dog. She claims that thar's some more of them little tinklin' birds in thar. I don't like 'em. Make a dog learn to hunt too slow. 'Spose yer step in thar an' let 'em have it on the nose. I've got number sixes in my gun."

I had number sixes in my gun. And Dud knew it. We all use sixes for grouse in this heavy country. Our birds are seldom caught out of thick cover. And our first shots, from old apple trees, in thickets, or at the edge of such cover, or from thorn-plum bushes, are apt to be snap shots. So all in all, we like number sixes. But I switched to number eights. And then I stepped in ahead of Lady G. Sure enough, another woodcock climbed to the top of the alders, and began to whistle about freedom. I caught him at about that moment.

"Good on your head," said Dud. "Go an' fetch fer Mak, Lady."

"Say, Dud," I said as we moved on, "this is a great dog."

"Well, crotch, Bart never sent me anythin' but good dogs. That seems to be what he raises. But I wish that this one was a little more peeticler. I like a dog that won't bother 'ith them fly-by-nighters. Like to have 'em specialize in pa'tridges. Of course, these little whistle-britches birds is all right. I'd rather gun fer them than saw wood."

Lady G. started up the path, through the alders. Again she halted, and her tail came up. It was a beautiful picture—the dog in that shadow and sun spotted path. She was pointing a bird in a thicket of alders that filled the wet ditch and sprawled over the bank to the second growth beyond the old pasture wall. Dud clutched my elbow, and we both halted in our tracks.

"Look at that, "Dud whispered. "Steady as the rock of ages, an' as purty as a wild thing in the month of May."

"Take that bird on the hop," I whispered.

"Aya. But as the little girl said, I hate to go above yer."

A round ball of russet feathers suddenly leaped into the air, and shot up straight for the sky and into the sun. The trim little twenty-gauge barked, and the bird fell, almost where it had started. And that was enough to start two more. One climbed in orthodox fashion. The other slanted off on a confusion of wings. Dud dropped the first with his second barrel. And I managed to spill the third.

"Crotch," exclaimed Dud, pushing his felt hat back on his head. "Now do yer suppose that bitch will look at us, like maybe we was one of her crowd?"

While he picked up the woodcock, I talked with his dog. Dud's muttering interrupted me. "Dang it all, I knew them things warn't worth shootin'. Look how small they be. I've shot pa'tridges year in an' year out, man an' boy, but it's been years since I cracked one of these tooters. It's kinda fun, ain't it?"

Evidently there were no more woodcock in that particular cover. The setter went to work on her own.

"Where d'ye figger them pa'tridges is, Mak?"

Of course, I wasn't expected to answer that question. But we finally located the plum bushes, about an old stone heap, that I had in mind. The dog was out of sight. Dud called. And with simply delightful manners, the setter obeyed the soft summons.

"Steady, Lady," said Dud, and we started in.

Catching bird scent, the setter raced ahead, and we lost sight of her for a moment.

"Now, we'll git a crack at sunthin' real, maybe," grinned Dud.

The grin was youthful. It would have fitted the face of a ten-year-old. Such is October's wizardry. And that is the big reason for gunning. For that, October days were made. So, for a few hours, at least, one may rub off the years.

Although there was bird scent in and about the thorn plums, there were no birds. They had been there earlier in the day. Morning and evening are the hours for such spots. The dog settled down to find those birds. By that time, I looked upon her as an old friend. In fact, I watched her work with open-mouthed admiration. It seemed to me that she was one in a million. To have been able to buy her at any price one could raise would have been a piece of unmitigated luck.

Dud watched me closely. And it certainly seemed to me that some hidden amusement betrayed itself in his face. At last he spoke.

"I know what ye're thinkin', Mak. It seems to you that this Lady G. is medium good. But she's jist another of Bart's dogs, I guess. All in all, I've shot over ten er fifteen of 'em. They've all been pa'tridge dogs. But thar was only one in the lot, a red Irisher, that was far an' away the best. Of course I remember them all, although I never tried to remember their hifalutin names. But the pitchur of the Irisher is hung in my heart. That's how I always let the rest of 'em go back at the end of the season, 'ithout too much trouble. I've liked 'em all, but danged if I didn't love that Irisher."

We were hurrying across an old field, knee-deep with dead June grass. The latest dog had raced across to thick cover beyond an old cedar fence. There wasn't much time to ponder on what Dud had said, but it did awaken an old curiosity. We had often wondered about these setters that belonged to a man referred to as Bart. Dud had let us wonder. Or perhaps it had never occurred to him that we wondered.

I for one had not intended to pry into a matter which he apparently chose to keep to himself. Still, one couldn't down the curiosity. This Bart—what sort of a fellow was he? The annual dog was always a perfectly trained animal. And although they certainly never lost anything of finish under Dud's hands, he never attempted to alter their education in the least. This Bart apparently loaned the dogs to Dud. It was, seemingly, an unusual gesture of friendship. Thus far, I had let it go at that. Now, for the moment, it had looked as though my old curiosity might be satisfied after all. When it became clear that Dud was not going to enlighten me after all, I suddenly determined to ask a question.

"Confound it all, Dud, who is this Bart?"

"Huh? Oh, he's one of them fellers that makes a livin', somehow, raisin' dogs . . . setters."

"Would you mind telling me what his last name is?"

"What? Do yer mean to say that I never mentioned his last name?"

"I don't think that you ever mentioned his last name, to me."

"Huh, that's funny. It's Brown—jist Brown, Bart Brown."

"I suppose that you and he have been hunting together a great deal?"

"Nope. I never saw him but once in my life. Though he's always promisin' that he'll be up fer some trout fishin'."

"Wait a minute," I said, as we came to the cedar fence. "I don't get this at all. Did you have the first dog, the Irisher, on trial? Hang it all, Dud, there's something in this succession of good bird dogs that is fantastic. Excuse me, but I've held in on it as long as I can."

Dud let the matter hang in the air, figuratively speaking, and sadly surveyed a tear in his woolen trousers.

"Bob-wire," he said, "is like a bankrupt's friends. It bobs up an' snatches what it can git hold of, 'ith no more decency than dynamite. Nancy will comment on this. Crotch! What was yer sayin'? No, I never had the Irish dog on trial. If thar had been any chance to buy that dog, I'd have bought him, if doin' so had ruined me now an' eternally. I'll help yer understand jist how much of a dog he was: Nancy would have taken in washing, to have kept that dog in our house. If we didn't have important business to transact, t'other side of the fence, I'd set right down an' tell yer the whole story. As 'tis, thar's jist erbout time to say that I had to return the Irisher to his rightful owner. He was a stolen dog."

"Stolen!" I gasped, not comprehending how Dud and Nancy could have been mixed up in an affair like that.

"Yes, sir, stolen. I got a black eye out of that rumpus. An' I don't know but that Nancy w'ud tell yer to this day that I got erternally disgraced in the course of events. But I d'know . . . I got a brand new setter to use, every year so long's I want one, er so long as Bart an' me can kick the leaves off the toe of our boots. An' if ye're still curious, I d'know but that I'll tell yer the rest of it sometime. But jist now, let's git over this danged fence."

XII

DUD'S IRISHER

AFTER the first hunt with the Latest Dog, Dud and I went home, riding through the softened colors of the late afternoon. While we were going down Babbit Ridge into the Bingham valley, deep with early October shadows, Dud began the story of the Irish setter. And the last light of the sunset lay on the western hills—Fletcher Mountain, and, far away, the blue peaks of Bigelow.

"This latest setter is a great dog," I said with conviction.

"Gosh, I'm afraid ye're right. An' I'm gittin' too old to be huntin' with a different dog every October. Still, I 'spose I'd better ship her back. A man puts his heart out to loan, when he keeps a dog."

"I know that. But why in the world should you ship her back, if it's down in the books that you don't need to? This is an outstanding bitch."

"Wel-el, she ain't the Irisher, yer know."

"Let's have that story," I said.

Dud chuckled. "Funny that it never occurred to me that yer didn't understand this dog situation as well as I did myself. It all happened a few years before you came round these parts. I keep fergittin' that yer ain't a native."

"Thanks for the compliment," I said.

"The crux of the situation, as Doc Brownin' w'ud say, is the Irisher. One day, 'bout fifteen years ago, I came down the street to git some fixings fer Nancy. When I got down in front of Preble an' Robinson's store, I see Doc Brownin' talking to a big, red Irisher, that was settin' on the runnin' board of a car with N'York license plates.

" 'Hello, Dud,' says Doc. 'Take a look at this Irish setter. Don't he look like he'd fit inter a patch of red an' yellow woods?'

"Doc was kinda soft on dogs an' hosses. He'd rather have a dog than sunthin' to eat. But his wife never felt jist that way. 'Crotch,' says Doc to me, 'if it warn't as undignified as huggin' a strange woman, I'd jist like to put my arms around this dog. He looks like an old friend, gol-durn him.'

"The Irisher kept to hisself, but his big tail swung back an' forth on the runnin' board. Bineby, a man comes out of the store, all dressed up in them rigs that they wear when they go bouncin' little balls over a mowed lot. He hardly glanced at Doc an' me. Jist strutted right by us, cranked his engine, an' climbed inter the car.

"I thought that was mighty peculiar, becuz it ain't no way fer a man that owns a dog like that to act. At least a word of greetin', an' a bit of biography, w'ud have been proper. The big car started with a jerk, when that feller let in the clutch. The dog had been lookin' at Doc an' me, so off he goes. Doc yelled, 'Hey Mister, your red dog is overboard!'

"The brakes squealed, an' when the car stopped, that feller stuck out a scowlin' face. When he'd taken in the situation, he called the dog in a nasty tone of voice. Yer c'ud see that the dog hated to mind him but he obeyed—walkin', not runnin'. I 'spose that provoked the feller, becuz he got out, an' when the dog came up to him, he kicked him full in the face. As Doc explained afterwards, when he was tryin' to make Nancy see how I come to git a black eye, it was simply incomprehensible how that feller kicked that dog.

" 'Damnation!' says Doc.

"Yer know, Doc was famous from one end of the county to the other fer his quick temper. He usually let it go the same way a person lets go of a hot dish.

" 'Well?' says the man with the short pants.

" 'By cripes, stranger!' says Doc, an' stopped becuz he c'udn't seem to select the next word.

" 'Yah? Well, what erbout it?'

" 'What erbout it!' says Doc, still strugglin' to speak nothin' but simple English. 'Why, damn your no-account yeller hide; damn your turned-up pants; an' your blasted soul! Fer half a cent I'd splatter that smirk off your ugly face. What right have you to a dog like that? A two-legged skunk like you be ain't fit to keep a snake.'

" 'So what's next?' says the feller, slow an' sarcastic. Then he turns on the dog. 'Git back in your place, Pete, or I'll kick the face off yer!'

"The dog climbed back on the runnin' board, like he was told to do.

" 'Thar,' says the man, 'how d'ye like them fer apples? Or maybe ye'd like a sample of what the dog got. Of course I'm in a hurry, but—'

"Now I've got to admit, Mak," interpolated Dud, "that all this sounds like what Nancy called it. 'Fantastic,' she kept sayin', until I give up tryin' to make her understand jist what did happen to Doc an' me. It's the way it happened, anyway. If the whole thing hadn't been so sudden an' upsettin', I think I w'ud have seen how crotchly re-diculous it was. But that ain't to be construed as an apology on my part.

"Yer see, while that feller was crackin' out his so-whats, Doc's eyes kept gittin' darker an' darker, like lakes under a November sky. Finally, he didn't seem to be payin' any attention to the blessin' he was gittin,' but to be anxiously lookin' up an' down the street. I was jist a little puzzled, myself. When he seemed satisfied, he turned 'round to me, an' says, 'Thar ain't a gosh-danged woman in sight. I'm a-goin' to knock the tar out of this tough guy.'

" 'Huh!' says the feller by the car. 'I thought yer was lookin' fer a cop.'

"Doc ignored that, too. 'Dud,' he says, 'it can't hurt your

[164]

reputation any to hold my coat. I ain't had a chance to do any-thin' like this fer years—not since the P.I. nailed my rubbers to the floor of the office camp at Number Ten. I felt ashamed of that fer years, but this is goin' to be different.'

"The feller got the p'int. 'I'll say it's goin' to be different,' he says.

"Doc started to take off his coat. Erbout then, that feller got inter action. It was an uppercut, an' it hit Doc where the feller aimed it. Doc didn't know a thing that happened fer the next few min-its. It was lucky that I didn't have no coat to take off.

"Anyhow, it w'ud have been a nice fight, I guess, if that setter hadn't got excited. When it jumped off the runnin' board, it got between that feller's legs. An' I warn't long in gettin' a-stride of the situation. The truth is, Mak, I was kinda mad. As I remember it, that was erbout the time Doc riz up an' felt of his jaw.

" 'What yer doin'?' he says to me.

" 'The enemy has been delivered inter my hands,' I says. 'And if I had on calkboots, I'd ride him. Thar ain't any women on the street, is thar?'

" 'Naw, thar ain't,' says Doc. 'Let him have it. An' give him one in the jaw fer me.'

"But I had got another fool idea in my head by that time. 'Mister,' I says, 'it w'udn't take any more'n a suggestion fer me to sp'il that arm of yours, way I've got it. I'm goin' to twist it up jist e-nough so's ye'll understand what I mean.' He let the blats out of him. 'Thar!' I says. 'Of course yer might roll out from under, but one arm w'udn't be much good to yer. In fact three arms w'udn't. Yer ain't goin' to kick that dog ag'in—'

[165]

" 'An' he ain't ever goin' to git a crack at my jaw ag'in,' adds Doc. 'The dirty, low-down frog sputter.'

" 'So,' I says, jist like I hadn't been interrupted, 'I'm goin' to buy that dog of yourn, or break your neck.' Of course, I didn't have hold of his neck, when I said that, but thar hain't no use in bein' pe-ticular, in a time like that.

" 'Doc,' I says, 'take that wallet out of my hip pocket. Put whatever money thar is in it over on the front seat of this feller's car. That is, if he's perfectly willin' to sell this dog to me.'

" 'Damn it,' says Doc. 'I'll buy this dog. I'll give twenty-five dollars.'

" 'No,' I says, 'he's doin' business 'ith *me*.' An' I give him jist a little mite of a twist fer emphasis. 'What d'yer say?'

"What he said was sartingly mixed with the earth-earthy, but he took me up, on my own terms, jist the same. Doc took the wallet from my pocket. When he come back from the car, he says, 'Thar warn't but seven dollars in it.'

"I stepped off quick, an' that was the fust I noticed that Doc had taken his coat off. The light of battle was poppin' in his eyes. But when he made a pass at that cuss, the feller jumped like a rabbit. The engine in his car had been runnin' all that time, so he got away. Doc was all cut up erbout missin' his chance.

"We sot down tergether on the curb. 'Dud,' says Doc, sort of soberin', 'maybe this dog ain't worth so much as a pie-eyed crane on the night b'fore Christmas.'

" 'Maybe ye're right,' says I, lookin' at the Irisher. 'But seven dollars ain't goin' to sink the ship.'

" 'Huh!' says Doc. 'I'll say it ain't. Here's your wallet.'

"It seemed to me, when I took it, that thar was still sunthin'

[166]

in it. I looked, an' thar was jist seven dollars. 'What!' I says, 'he'll be back. Likely this will land us in jail.'

" 'By the right-hand toe of Heraclitus,' says Doc, 'I jist wish he w'ud come back.'

"So that's how I come by the Irisher."

"But I still don't see where Bart comes in."

"Crotch, Mak, of course yer don't. Hold your hosses. Anyway I begun this yarn w'ud have been back-end to, but Doc Brownin' uster say that some almighty smart men had been born that way.

"When I come to try out the Irisher, I found that he was so good that nobudy but Doc w'ud believe me. I challenge Noah Webster to find a fit word to describe that dog. But wait a min-it, *I had to go home*, after dickerin' with this feller in short pants.

"When me an' the Irisher come up over the hill, Nancy was jist comin' out of the back door with a saucer of milk fer her cat. That cat never got by on his principles. He never had any. An' he didn't git by on his manners, fer they was mostly bad; but he was neat—that is to say, he knew he'd better be—an' so he lived on the fat of the land.

"I guess the Irisher was purty hungry and thirsty, an' before I c'ud say anythin', he was racin' fer that milk. The cat saw him comin', an' went under the back stoop, like he'd seen the devil hisself. Nancy jist stood thar, wonderin' what on earth had got inter that cat, until she see the strange dog. Then she took four er five steps back'ards. The dog had got within two er three yards of her, b'fore she saw him. An' what do yer think that setter done?"

"My gosh," I gasped, "I don't dare guess."

"He stood right up on his hind legs, like a man, an' walked

[167]

towards her. Nancy jist gasped, an' set the saucer of milk down on the step, an' the dog warn't long in appropriating it."

"And then, what did Nancy say?"

"She says, 'Dudley! Whose dog is that?'

" 'Ours,' I says.

" '*Ours!*'

" 'Yes, marm,' I says. 'Ours.'

" 'Look at your eyes!' she says.

"An' that changed the subject.

"Next day er so, Doc an' I went out. Pa'tridges was as plentiful then as they be now in stories. Wing shots was apt to be easy, an' sometimes yer had to kick 'em in the tail to git any action at all, but mostly they did purty well, when they got the hang of the idea. The only thing a man needed a dog fer was the company an' extra exercise. Fer the most part, that Irisher showed that he was a past master at his trade. Tame pa'tridges puzzled him, but we stuck to the same birds day after day, an' they got so they hated our company. That made 'em harder fer Doc, who never was much of a wing shot.

"Wel-el, we sartinly had a lot of wholesome fun. It was too good to last—in a world like this. Like a rose. An' one night when I got home, I see that Nancy had been cryin' an' that meant that somebudy was dead, er as good as.

" 'Well,' I says, 'let me have both barrels between the eyes.'

"But all she done was hand me a paper.

" 'What's this?' I says, all in the fog.

" 'That,' she says, p'intin' at an advertisement.

"An' thar it was! It was a complete description of the Irisher. Said that it was believed he had been stolen, an' that thar was

[168]

a reward of one hundred dollars, no questions asked. An' somewhere in it, I see that the dog's name was Peter Perfect. The Irisher was lyin' in front of the kitchen stove, which, by the way, had always been the cat's favorite mat. He was pullin' an' tuggin' at a burdock burr in his tail, when I spoke to him. 'Peter,' I says, an' he jist erbout tipped the stove over.

" 'I guess that settles it,' I says to Nancy.

" 'The train leaves at six o'clock tomorrow mornin',' she says.

"An' fer once in my life, I completely misjedged my woman.

" 'Damn the reward!' I says.

" 'Of course,' she says, 'but that man loves this dog. An' it's *his* dog.'

" 'Well, blast it!' I says. 'I'll take the six o'clock. I ain't goin' to ship this Irisher by no express. 'Sides that, I'm goin' to be sure erbout the rightful owner. To git this dog, I had one fight, an' I don't know but that I c'ud stand another.'

" 'I'll go with you,' says Nancy.

"I see thar was tears in her eyes. They run down her face, an' splashed on the Irisher's head. That was the fust I noticed that he'd gone over an' put his head in Nancy's lap.

"So we took the six o'clock ... headed fer a place outside of Portland. When we got thar, thar was another woman in the pitchur. The Irisher was that kind of a dog. Even Doc's wife took to him. Nancy an' Bart's wife was good friends from the fust look at each other. They cried a little, which was dum foolish. Bart started peelin' out his wallet, to pay me the reward. I was so mixed up, what 'ith them women sort of blubbing an' the happy way the Irisher acted, that I didn't pay much attention to what Bart was doin', an' I don't know but that I'd have put his money in my pocket, if Nancy hadn't fetched out one of them 'Dudleys!' of her'n.

"Wel-el, when them Browns see how the wind was blowin', they took us round back of the house. An' thar was all kinds of setters. An' in one yard, thar was a littlish bitch with a whole litter of red pups.

" 'They're Peter Perfect's pups,' explains Mrs. Bart.

" 'Take your pick,' says Bart.

"I looked at Nancy, an' she nodded fer me to go ahead. Then I looked at the Irisher, who had followed us. I suppose that it w'ud have been natural to take one of them pups, but by crotch all of a sudden I knew that I didn't want no more red dogs, unless—I think that Bart got the idea, but that Mrs. Bart was disappointed in me.

" 'I'll give yer two hundred dollars fer the Irisher,' I says.

"It was a lot of money, Mak. Nancy's chest kinda breathed hard, but I see that she was with me.

" 'We're sorry, honest,' says Bart, 'but how can we run a dog farm without Peter Perfect?' An' his wife looked terrible anxious.

" 'Tell yer what,' says Bart, 'I'll send yer one of my best dogs, when the bird shootin' comes round next fall. If yer like him, keep him—no charge. If yer don't like him, specially, ship him back. Thar'll be one fer yer, every fall, so long as I'm in the business.'

"So that's how it come erbout—that's how it happened that all the dogs he's loaned me has been Englishers. I told him, 'All right, but ye're not to send any *red dogs.*' "

That was the end of the story. During the last of it, we had been sitting in the car, outside Dud's yard. As Dud finished, the latest dog put her nose on his shoulder. The old veteran shot a sideways look at me, and grinned.

"And so—" I suggested.

"An' so . . . wel-el, I d'know. I see Nancy givin' this dog some milk in the cat's saucer, this mornin'. I d'know."

"Do you think that your friend Bart would sell this dog?"

"Crotch no! This ain't *his* dog—no more."

"Good night, Dud."

"Night, Mak. Come on, Lady G."